TEACHERS OF INDIA

TEACHERS OF INDIA

C. A. KINCAID

GYAN

Published by

Gyan Publishing House
5, Ansari Road
Daryaganj, New Delhi-110002
Phone: 011-47034999, 9811692060
E-mail: books@gyanbooks.com

Distribution Network
gyanbooks.com
India, USA, Canada, UK, Australia

ISBN: 978-93-7014-068-4 (PB)

First Published, 1927

2nd Impression 2025

Printed at: Gyan Press, Delhi.

TEACHERS OF INDIA
Author: C. A. KINCAID

BOOKS BY THE SAME AUTHOR

The Indian Heroes.

Tales from the Indian Epics.

Tales from the Indian Drama.

A History of the Maratha People, 3 Vols.

Tales of King Vikrama.

Tales of Old Sind.

Tales of the Saints of Pandharpur.

The Anchorite.

TEACHERS OF INDIA

BY

C. A. KINCAID, C.V.O., I.C.S.

Officier de L'instruction Publique

Author of 'A History of the Maratha People,' 'Ishtur Phakde,' 'The Indian Heroes,' 'Tales from the Indian Epics,' 'The Tale of the Tulsi Plant,' 'Deccan Nursery Tales,' etc., etc.

HUMPHREY MILFORD

OXFORD UNIVERSITY PRESS

LONDON BOMBAY CALCUTTA MADRAS

1927

To Shrimant
Meherban Sir Chintamanrao Patwardhan, K.C.I.E.,
Chief of Sangli
As a Slight Tribute of High Regard and Esteem
This Book
is
Affectionately Inscribed.

PREFACE

IN this the last book that I shall publish in India, I have sketched the careers of a number of persons, who, although they led strictly religious lives, yet played, unknown to themselves, a great part in the History of India. The Maratha saints inspired the Maratha empire. Kabir was the originator of Akbar's attempt to secure Hindu and Musulman unity. To the Sikh gurus the Sikh kingdom owed more than to Maharaja Ranjit Singh. The Guzarat poets Mirabai and Narsinh Mehta and their successors were not the cause of any military movement; but they certainly helped to make the Guzarati what he is to-day—the clearest-headed business man in all India. Nor was their inspiration absent from the Rajput resistance in Kathiawar both to Musulmans and Marathas. The historian of the future will certainly reckon the Arya Samaj as the greatest force in the modern agitation (I use the word in no invidious sense) against English rule.

C. A. K.

CONTENTS

INTRODUCTION

THE story of the teachers of the Deccan will be found in Mahipati's *Bhaktavijaya*, which I have repeatedly read in the original Marathi. I have given a fuller account of their doings in my book, *Saints of Pandharpur* (Oxford University Press); but I have therein treated the subject differently. I am greatly indebted to Mr. Nadkarni's *A Short History of Marathi Literature*, an admirable book, as concise as it is valuable. I have tried to obtain leave from Mr. Nadkarni to borrow from his work, but I have failed to communicate with him. I trust that, if he reads this book, he will forgive me for my pilfering.

The story of Kabir will be found in Mahipati's *Bhaktavijaya* and in the Introduction to Kabir's poems by Mr. Rabindranath Tagore. Permission to make use of Mr. Tagore's translations of two of the poems has been courteously given me by Messrs. Macmillan & Co.

The story of the Teachers of Guzarat is taken from Mahipati and also from a most valuable work, *Milestones in Guzarati Literature*, written by Mr. Jhaveri, Chief Judge of the Small Cause Court of Bombay. He was so very good as to place its contents at my disposal. I have also to thank Mr. Mehta, Assistant Judge of Ahmedabad, for his energetic and most valuable help in supplying me with Guzarati materials, of which I have made the fullest use.

The story of the Sikh Gurus is taken chiefly from the late Mr. Macauliffe's *The Sikh Religion.* I find it difficult adequately to express my appreciation of the greatest and noblest work ever written by an Englishman in India. Most writers on religion are prompted by a feeling that they will receive some handsome compensation, if not in this life, at any rate hereafter. Mr. Macauliffe needed no such stimulus. He spent his life, his private means, his health, in the sympathetic interpretation and study of a religion of which he was not a follower. All honour to him! I have to thank the Clarendon Press for kindly allowing me to dip with both hands into *The Sikh Religion*. Other authorities consulted by me were *Ramanand to Ram Tirth*, published by Messrs. G. A. Natesan & Co., of Madras, *The Sikkhan de Raj de Vikhia*, Dr. Trumpp's *Adi Granth*, Cunningham's *Sikhs*, and *The Sikhs* by General Sir John Gordon.

For the story of Dayanand Saraswati I have consulted *Ramanand to Ram Tirth* and Farquhar's *Modern Religious Movements in India.* For my sketch of Keshab Chandra Sen, my authority is his life by Muzumdar, kindly lent me by Mr. Motiram Advani of Haidarabad. Much of this book has already appeared in the *Times of India* (weekly illustrated) and in the *Daily Gazette of Karachi*. I have to thank the editors of these papers for their courteous permission to reprint it.

C. A. K.

TEACHERS OF THE DECCAN

1. Dnyandev

Although Mukundraj was earlier than Dnyandev, still as none of Mukundraj's verses have survived in the form in which he wrote them, it may fairly be said that Dnyandev was the earliest Marathi poet whose work is extant. He was certainly the first of the Pandharpur school of poets.

The tale how Pandharpur came to be regarded as holy is a strange one. It is now a town on the lower reaches of the Bhima River, but in early times it was a thick forest called Dandirvan. In the forest lived two old people, Janudev and his wife Satyavati. They had an undutiful son known as Pundalik ; and Pundalik and his wife so illtreated his parents, that they resolved to go on a pilgrimage. When their daughter-in-law heard of it, she insisted on going also. She and Pundalik rode with the other pilgrims, while Janudev and Satyavati walked. In the evening the poor old couple, dead tired although they were, had to groom Pundalik's and his wife's horses. They soon regretted their decision to go on a pilgrimage. Their release was near at hand. One evening the body of pilgrims stopped for the night at the hermitage of a sage called Kukutswami. All fell asleep except Pundalik. As he lay awake, he saw several ill clad but lovely women enter Kukutswami's hermitage, clean the floor, fetch water and wash his clothes. They then went into the hermit's room and came out beautifully clad. The wicked Pundalik threw himself at the women's feet and asked them who they were. They replied that they were the Ganges, the Yamuna, and other sacred rivers, wherein pilgrims used to bathe. Their clothes were soiled because of the pilgrims' sins, but they became clean again through Kukutswami's virtues. They then rated Pundalik as the worst sinner of them all, because of his treatment of his parents. Pundalik's nature changed completely. From the most cruel he became the most devoted of sons and by his kindness to his parents, he induced them to return to Dandirvan. One day the god Krishna, who had come southwards from Dwarka, wished to see Pundalik. The latter was in attendance on his parents. He refused to leave them even at a god's wish. He threw a brick outside the door for Krishna to stand on, while he waited. His work over, Pundalik went outside and excused himself to Krishna. The god so far from being angry praised Pundalik and bade Pundalik worship him ever afterwards as Vithoba or Him, who stood on a brick.

In this spot hallowed by sacred legends, Dnyandev made his abode and was the first of a long line of poets. His father was one Vithoba of Apegaon, called after the god of Pandharpur. He had no children and in a fit of religious melancholy, he left his wife Rakhmai and became an anchorite at Benares. To leave a childless wife and become an anchorite is wrong; and when Vithoba's preceptor heard of Rakhmai, he sent Vithoba back to her. Of their subsequent union four children were born, Nivratti, Dnyandev, Sopana, and Muktabai.

Vithoba's return to the world offended the Brahmans of Alandi, a town on the Indryani River where Vithoba had gone to live. They outcasted Vithoba and would not invest the eldest son Nivratti with the sacred thread. Vithoba and Rakhmai fled in disgust to Prayag, leaving their children to fend for themselves. The children pleaded to the Alandi Brahmans that they had committed no sin. The Brahmans so far relented as to promise to invest them with the sacred thread, if they got a letter of purification from Paithan, a holy place on the Godavari. Nivratti, therefore and his two brothers and his sister Muktabai went to Paithan. There the Paithan Brahmans mocked them and told them to prostrate themselves before every dog, pig, hare, ass, cow, that they met. A buffalo just then came up. The Brahmans gave it the name of Dnyandev (God of Wisdom) to which name, so they said, it was as much entitled as the boy from Alandi. Dnyandev agreed and putting his hand on the buffalo's head made it recite correctly the four Vedas. This and other miracles convinced the Brahmans of Paithan. They gave Nivratti a letter of purification and the Alandi Brahmans invested him and his two brothers with the sacred thread.

After this victory Dnyandev began his work as a poet. His greatest book was the Dnyaneshwari, a translation of, and a Marathi commentary of, the *Bhagwat Gita*. It contains more than 9,000 couplets. The original *Gita* contains only 700. The following passage translated by Mr. Nadkarni is typical of the whole :

'My Friend ! Why need you purity of birth? . . . If there be no devotion to me (Krishna), it is worthless. A cornfield full of empty ears, a deserted town, a dry lake are all valueless. So too is a tree that flowers, but yields no fruit.'

Besides the Dnyaneshwari Dnyandev wrote the Amritanbhav a poem that gives an abstract of the *Upanishads*. His brother Sopana wrote some verses. Muktabai was also a considerable poetess. Once Dnyandev, angry with her for some cause or another, refused to see her and shut himself up in his room, Muktabai, then only fifteen, wrote a charming *abhang* or short poem, begging him to open his door.

> 'Forgive me Dnyaneshwar and open the door!
> 'He who would be a saint must bear with the words of other men.
> 'He has greatness who has no pride.
> 'Where greatness dwells there dwells mercy also.
> 'With whom should one be angered? All of us are Brahma the All-pervading.
> 'Look all round you, Dnyaneshwar and open the door!
> 'An anchorite has a pure mind, so he suffers from the sins of others.
> 'If the world is on fire, the water to quench it must come from the mouths of the saints.
> 'If the saint is hurt by sharp edged words, he must accept them as good counsel.
> 'The world is evolved from Para Brahma—Dnyaneshwar open the door!'

Dnyandev, his brothers and sister died when hardly more than children. They seem all to have had a curious longing for death, produced perhaps by the misfortunes of their country; for they lived about the time of the Afghan conquest of the Deccan. At the age of twenty-two, Dnyandev resolved to take *Samadhi,* in other words to bury himself alive at Pandharpur. The poet Namdev has told the end of Dnyandev in beautiful and touching verses. One day when Dnyandev, his brothers and sister were sitting at Pandharpur in the temple of Krishna, Dnyandev said that he wanted to be buried at the feet of the god's image. The god answered that if Dnyandev were buried at Pandharpur, his fame would be overshadowed by that of the god. He must be buried at Alandi. Dnyandev reluctantly consented on a promise that he should see Krishna at least once a year. At Alandi amid a rain of heavenly flowers, Dnyandev entered a grave that had been dug for him. A deerskin was spread for him to sit upon and a woodfire was lit in a fireplace made for that purpose. Inhaling the wood-smoke, Dnyandev became slowly unconscious. While he lay in a stupor, his disciples sealed the mouth of the grave. Not long afterwards Sopana had himself buried alive at Saswad near Purandar Fort and Nivratti at Trimbakeshwar in the Nasik District. Muktabai vanished in a lightning flash on the banks of the Tapti River.

A stately fane was built to mark the spot where Dnyandev passed away and Alandi and Saswad and Trimbak are well-known places of pilgrimage. Nor was the promise of the god Krishna unfulfilled. Every Kartak Sud 11 (October) a great crowd of pilgrims take Dnyandev's image in a palanquin from Alandi to Pandharpur. A fortnight later (Kartak Wad 11) the pilgrims bear the image in its palanquin back to Alandi from Pandharpur. Nor does the great saint go unhonoured; for invisible to human eyes the god Krishna, so the pilgrims believe, walks alongside the palanquin to return the visit of his beloved disciple. Nay more; it is now generally believed that Nivratti, Dnyandev, Sopana and Muktabai were not ordinary mortals, but were respectively the incarnations of the gods Shiva, Vishnu, Brahmadev and of the goddess Laxmi. This the poet Mahipati has stated as an undisputed fact and Moropant has reiterated it in the following fine couplet :—

'Shankar, Nivratti, Hari, tu, Dnyanesh, Brahmadev Sopan.
'Vidhya Mukhta; tumchya kirtisudhechen sada aso pan.'

[Nivratti was Shankar (Shiva). You, O Dnyandev were Hari (Vishnu). Sopana was Brahmadev. Muktabai was Vidhya. May your fame endure for ever and ever !]

TEACHERS OF THE DECCAN

2. Chokhamela: the Mhar Poet

One of Dayandev's earliest followers was a Mhar called Chokhamela. His father and mother Sudama and Muktabai lived at Anagod near Pandharpur. They were rich as Mhars go. They owned no less than half the Mhar watan lands of the village; but they were childless and therefore unhappy. To obtain a son Sudama made no less than two hundred and forty-four pilgrimages to Pandharpur. One day in her husband's absence, it fell to Muktabai to convey two hundred mangoes from the Mhar lands to be divided by the Musulman governor of Bedar.

As Muktabai walked, a starving Brahman met her and asked for some mangoes. She at first refused, because, until the Musulman governor had divided the fruit, she could not give even her own share away. The Brahman fell on the ground and vowed that he would die unless he got some food. In despair the kind-hearted Muktabai gave him five mangoes. The hungry man ate them all and blessed her, 'You gave me five mangoes,' he said, 'you shall therefore have five children. Call the eldest Chokha, because I have sucked (*chokhanen*) the mangoes.' With these words the Brahman vanished. When Muktabai reached Bedar the governor's clerk reported that she had come very late and that instead of two hundred she had brought two hundred and fifty mangoes. The governor sent for her and asked her explanation. She told her story. The governor, although of another faith, was yet a pious man and let her go in peace. He believed her and guessed that she had fed a god and that he had repaid her gift tenfold.

In due course a son was born to Muktabai and received the name of Chokha or Chokhamela. Trained by pious parents, he grew up a saintly boy. According to the legend, his piety brought him a rich reward. As a Mhar, it was his duty to drag the bodies of dead cattle away from the villagers' houses. One day he happened to be the only Mhar present in Anagod and it fell to him to drag away the body of a big cow that had just died. The task would ordinarily have been too great for the half-grown lad; but the god Krishna came to his aid. With the god's help he easily finished the task. When he had done it, a high-born maiden, who had been permitted to see the god, threw herself at Chokhamela's feet and implored him to accept her as his bride. So signal a proof of divine favour led Chokhamela to give up his home at Anagod and live in Pandharpur. As a Mhar, he could not enter the temples; but he prayed continuously to Shri Krishna from the outer gate. The thought of a Mhar saint, however, was too much for the local Brahmans; and the persecution that befell him forms the subject of one of Mahipati's most graceful poems. The gist of the poem is shortly this. One day as Chokhamela was praying to Shri Krishna from outside the temple courtyard, a Brahman sneered at him and said, 'Your prayers to Krishna are as likely to be heard as a dog's would be, who asked to eat

GOPAL-KRISHNA TEMPLE, GOPALPURA, PANDHARPUR

at the same table as a Brahman. A wanderer in the forest is more likely to find a Wishing Tree; a dying man is more likely to find a jar filled with ambrosia than you are to win the favour of Shri Krishna.' Chokhamela humbly protested that the sun made no difference between castes and that the god only deemed holy those who loved him. He then walked sadly away.

That night, however, the god himself came to console Chokhamela. He carried the Mhar saint through the unlocked doors of the temple and seated him by his own side in the innermost shrine. A Brahman priest witnessed the incident and called his brethren to see the dreadful spectacle of a Mhar seated in the holy of holies. They drove Chokhamela out of the temple and made him live on the far side of the Bhima River. There the unhappy Mhar built a *dipmala* or stone lamp-stand in honour of Shri Krishna and prayed continuously towards the Pandharpur temple of which he could only see the distant spires. One day the god honoured Chokhamela by dining with him and his wife. A priest heard the Mhar saint addressing Shri Krishna, whom the priest because of his worldliness could not see. The priest thought that Chokhamela did this to slight the god. In a great rage he rushed at the unfortunate Mhar and struck him a violent blow on the face. Then he washed to clean himself of the pollution of touching a Mhar and went to pray at Krishna's shrine. To his horror, he saw the face of the image swollen and bleeding on the very spot where he had struck Chokhamela. Realizing from the miracle, that Chokhamela was a beloved disciple of the god, he went back across the Bhima and, taking the Mhar by the hand, led him back into the temple.

The end of Chokhamela was tragic. In A.D. 1332 the governor of Bedar impressed all the Mhars in his province to build a protecting wall round Mangalvedha town. Chokhamela was impressed with the others. When the work was all but finished, part of the wall fell and crushed a number of workmen, including the saint. For many years his remains lay unhonoured beneath the fallen ruins. After his death, however, his reputation as a saint steadily grew. At last the tailor poet Namdev received at Pandharpur a divine message to carry to Krishna's temple the bones of the poor Mhar. Namdev went to Mangalvedha; but Chokhamela's bones were mingled with those of several hundred fellow-workmen. At first Namdev was at a loss to identify those that he sought. At last placing his ear to the ground, he heard at one spot the cry of 'Vithoba! Vithoba!'—He knew that the bones that lay there were Chokhamela's. Reverently Namdev collected them and took them to Pandharpur. A stone still stands to mark the spot where he buried them.

In one sense Chokhamela can hardly be deemed a teacher; for although he wrote many verses, very few have survived. But the rise of a Mhar to sainthood taught a lesson of humility to the higher castes and of encouragement to the lower ones. The *dipmala* that he built still stands across the Bhima River; and when the palanquin of the god Krishna as Vithoba is every month taken round Pandharpur, it stops at the *dipmala* that floral offerings may be duly made at the saint's former dwelling place. The stone, too, where his remains were buried, is always pointed out to the curious visitor; and from it the Mhars to-day worship the god, without let or hindrance. For the god proved by his favour to Chokhamela that in his eyes caste is of little value. All that counts is *Bhakti* or true devotion.

TEACHERS OF THE DECCAN

3. Eknath

Eknath was a Deshast Brahman and was born at Paithan on the Godavari in A.D. 1548. This was an important period in the history of Maharashtra. The Bahmani empire had broken up into five smaller kingdoms, all of which were at constant war with each other. Eknath's great grandfather Bhanudas had been a famous saint of Pandharpur and had recovered from Anegundi the image of Vithoba, taken there by King Krishnaraya of Vijayanagar. Eknath's father Suryanarayan and his mother Rukminibai died when Eknath was still a child and he was brought up by his grandfather Chakrapani. The latter was a pious old man who taught Eknath to read and write and to understand the Vedas. Inspired by his ancestor's example and Chakrapani's teaching, Eknath formed the wish to be a saint like Bhanudas. One day while in a temple, he heard a voice tell him to go to Devgiri or Daulatabad and become there the pupil of Janardan Swami.

This Janardan Swami was the minister of the Barid Shahi king of Bedar. He was so saintly a man that the Musulman king allowed him to take a holiday every Thursday, so as to worship the god Dattatraya, whom he specially followed. Eknath reached Daulatabad in a few days and found the minister absorbed in official business. At first Janardan Swami paid no attention to the boy standing respectfully in front of him. At last he asked him what he wanted. When he heard that the boy had walked all the way from Paithan to Daulatabad to beg for religious instruction, Janardan's heart was touched and he made Eknath his pupil. Eknath faithfully repaid the minister's kindness. One day, so the story runs, a hostile force appeared outside Daulatabad to waste the countryside. The king ordered Janardan Swami to collect some troops and drive away the raiders. It was a Thursday and Janardan Swami was in a holy trance, reflecting on the qualities of the god Dattatraya. Sooner than disturb his master, Eknath assumed his duties. He collected an armed body and led them sword in hand against the enemy. He beat them off with great slaughter. He then returned to tell his master ; but the Swami was still absorbed in religious contemplation. When the Guru returned to things mundane, he was delighted to learn that his young pupil had done all that he himself could have done, had he been in a normal state.

It was several years before Janardanswami thought Eknath fit for *upadesh* or complete initiation. One day Eknath, whom Janardan had made his accountant, was unable to square his daily accounts. The missing sum was a single paise, but Eknath sat poring over his books until 3 a.m. When he discovered the error, he was so pleased that he clapped his hands with joy. This act awoke the Swami. On hearing that the boy had sat up nearly all night to trace a single paise, he felt that Eknath could safely be initiated to the full knowledge, that he himself possessed. 'If you give your mind,' he said to his pupil, 'as devotedly to the study of God as you have to my accounts, you will surely attain to perfect knowledge.'

After receiving the *upadesh* from Janardan, Eknath went to the holy places of India in turn— Benares, Prayag, Ayodhya, Dwarka and others. Then he went back at Janardan's bidding to Paithan and rejoined his grandfather Chakrapani. There he married Girjabai, the daughter of a Brahman of Bijapur and became a religious teacher. He spent the rest of his life preaching at Paithan until his death in A.D. 1609. He left behind him a son, Hari Pandit and through him he became the ancestor of the great poet Mukteshwar.

Many are the popular tales repeated of Eknath. On one occasion no less a person than the god Dattatraya dined with him and his master Janardan Swami. As was to be expected in one of the Pandharpur school of poets, Eknath was a devout worshipper of the god Krishna. It is said that it was he who first made popular in the Deccan the celebration of the Gokul Ashtami, the anniversary of the god Krishna's birth.

Eknath was a foe to caste distinctions. One day he was celebrating the *shradh* or anniversary celebration of his father's death and was waiting for the coming of the Brahmans whom he had invited. Some starving Mhars happened to pass by and the smell of the banquet reached their noses. Eknath overheard them lamenting that although they could smell such good food, they had no hope of eating it. Eknath was touched at their humility and suffering. He told his wife Girjabai to give some of the food to the Mhars. She did so and fed not only the men but also their wives and children. When the Brahmans came and saw the Mhars eating part of their dinner, they were very angry and refused to sit down. This meant that the spirit of Eknath's father would not receive due honour. But Krishna appeared in the guise of a Brahman attendant and told Eknath to his surprise that he need not be troubled, as other Brahman guests would be forthcoming. A moment or two later Eknath's father, great-grandfather and grandfather appeared to the terror of the sulking Brahmans and ate up the remains of the dinner prepared for them.

The strangest tale of all is that told of Eknath and a Brahman called Dandwat Swami. This virtuous person used to show his humility by prostrating himself at full length before every man or beast that he met. Some worldly Brahmans asked him in mockery to prostrate himself before a dead ass. Dandwat Swami did so and—wonder of wonders!—the dead ass came to life. When Eknath heard of this miracle, he forbade Dandwat Swami to repeat it, as such miracles were not suited to the *Kaliyuga* or evil modern times. He further advised Dandwat Swami to die, as he was too virtuous for this world. Dandwat Swami thought the advice good. He plunged into a deep meditation and gradually passed away. The evil Brahmans of Paithan, who still smarted from the loss of their dinner, charged Eknath with the murder of Dandwat Swami and they refused to accept his explanation. They threatened him with death, unless he could make the stone bull in front of Shiva's temple at Paithan eat grass. This was a mere trifle for so great a saint. The stone bull on seeing the grass put out its tongue, gathered in the grass and ate it. The stone bull and the tombs of the ass and of Dandwat Swami are still pointed out to pilgrims at Paithan.

If Eknath had only been a preacher, he would long ago have been forgotten ; but he was also the greatest poet of what Mr. Nadkarni styles the second period of Marathi literature. Writing in the *ovi* metre—a simple metre rather like that of Campbell's 'Hohenlinden'—he wrote a number of long and highly esteemed poems of the stories of the Epics. The chief are the Eknathi Bhagwat, and the Rukmini Swayamwar. He revised carefully the Dyaneshwari. He wrote also a certain amount of didactic verse, of which the following quoted by Mr. Nadkarni affords a good example :

'My good Sir, you have become a Sanyasi, but your desires and your passions have not left you. Why did you spoil your life to no purpose.

'Be Wise.

'You renounced in vain your wife and your children, but you have not found God.

'Be Wise.

'You have shaven your head, you have broken your sacred thread and you have rent your dhoti; you have taken in your hand a pilgrim's staff.

'Be Wise.

'You repeat over and over again the word "Narayan" but you think all the time of carnal pleasures. Why then did you become an anchorite?

'Be Wise.'

'Keep now your thoughts on one object only. Mix only with saintly men. Eknath, the disciple of Janardan, gives you this advice.

'Be Wise.'

TEACHERS OF THE DECCAN

4. Tukaram

Of all Marathi poets there is none who has achieved such popularity as Tukaram. His father was one Boloji, a petty grocer of Dehu Village, fourteen miles north-east of Poona. He was descended from a pious ancestor called Vishwambhar, who built a temple to Krishna and Rukmini on the banks of the Indrayani River. Tukaram, born in A.D. 1607 was the second son of Boloji. His eldest brother Savji was an ascetic from his earliest years; so Boloba looked to Tukaram to help him carry on the business. When Tukaram was only thirteen, he was admitted to its secrets and for five years he was a great help to his father. Then his father and mother died. Bad years came and Tukaram's first wife Rakma and his little son Shivaji died of privations. Savji became a wandering anchorite and disappeared. Tukaram proved unequal to these repeated misfortunes. He gave up the family business and devoted himself to religion and especially to the worship of Krishna and Rukmini.

Tukaram had a second wife Avalai, whose name has become in Marathi the equivalent of a scold or termagant; but there is no doubt that, although at times a sore trial to Tukaram, she loyally worked for him and his children like a common labourer. Many are the stories told of their relations. One day when she was bathing, Tukaram gave away her clothes to a passing beggar. Another day Tukaram was employed by a farmer to scare birds from his crop. Tukaram, however, soon forgot his task and began dreaming of Shri Krishna and Rukmini. The birds, undisturbed, ate up the corn. When the farmer came back, he was furious. He dragged Tukaram to the village headman and made him pass a bond for two *khandis* of grain, a bumper crop. In exchange he could take over what corn the birds had left. Tukaram would have let them finish their work of destruction; but Avalai made him reap the crop. Shri Krishna pleased with his disciple's devotion, came to his help. The corn when reaped came to eighteen *khandis* or nine times the full produce of the field. Avalai looked forward to the enjoyment of this windfall; but Tukaram, after paying the farmer, spent the rest in restoring the temple built by his ancestor Vishwambhar.

Avalai made a last effort to give Tukaram a fresh start. She borrowed from her father two hundred rupees, bought some goods and sent Tukaram out with some hawkers that he might sell them. At Supa, unfortunately, Tukaram saw a poor Brahman driven from his home by his creditors. He at once paid the Brahman's debts by handing over his own stock in trade. On his return to Dehu, the villagers decided that he was a madman. They mounted him on a donkey and paraded him through the streets with a string of onions round his neck. Tukaram fled from the villagers and hid in the Bambhunath hills. There his younger brother Kanhoba found him and brought him home. Kanhoba had grown to manhood and being of a practical mind wanted to start afresh the family business. They had no money, but they had bonds from various villagers and they were not all bad debts. Tukaram would have nothing to do with the bonds and when Kanhoba divided the bonds, Tukaram flung his share into the Indrayani. Having done this, he fled back to the Bambhunath hills. There the faithful Avalai sought and found him. She no doubt scolded him well, but day after day she brought him his food. One morning a thorn entered her foot; yet faint with pain she took her husband his meal as usual. This so touched Tukaram that he went back with her to Dehu. He could not, however, return to his grocery. While he lived among the hills, he had seen in a dream the god Krishna and the poet Namdev coming towards him. 'Pure saint, awake,' said the god, 'for I have brought you in Namdev a friend and admirer. When he was on earth, he made a vow to write a hundred million lines. He had only written 94,400,000 lines when he was called away to Vishnu's heaven. It is for you to write the remaining 5,600,000. I shall help you and bless you and you shall succeed.' When sleep left Tukaram, he felt a poet's inspiration and he began the long series of his poems, that only ended with his life. His metre was the simple *abhang* metre, but the effect of his poems has been finely described by the great poet Moropant.

'His (Tukaram's) *abhangs* pierce the heart of the wicked like the arrows of Rama. Just as the arrows of desire cannot pierce the heart of Shiva, so the words of others could not lead Tukaram astray. Tukaram knew the All-pervading Spirit as only King Janak knew it. So strict was his life that he made even Sanak, that Indra among sages, bow his head.'

Tukaram will chiefly be remembered by foreigners,

because of his association with the great Shivaji. The latter, who had a deep religious strain, was anxious to have near him some pious man from whom he might obtain religious instruction. He had tried to get Ramdas to live in his camp ; but Ramdas had refused. The king sent a messenger and a cavalry escort to fetch Tukaram. The saint felt that the camp of a high-spirited and warlike prince was no place for him. He wrote back the famous letter in verse, known to every educated man in Maharashtra ; I shall quote a few lines :—

> 'Torches, umbrellas and horses, these are not among the things that are good for me. Why, O lord of Pandhari, dost thou snare me with them. Honours, finery and aping others, I count as the filth of a pigstye. O God, says Tuka, run to set me free from these.
>
> 'If I came to your place, O king, seeking honours, what happiness should I find there? In the house of a king the wealthy are respected; the common herd meet with home. If I saw there fine raiment and jewels, I should die of it. If you scorn me when you hear this, still God will not scorn me. Let me tell you this and it will surprise you. There is no happiness like a beggar's. Austerity and renunciation are the greatest of things; wealthy men whose desires entangle them, are miserable. Tuka says that you are rich and honoured; but the followers of Hari are more fortunate.'

On receiving this letter Shivaji left his camp and actually joined Tukaram, becoming for the time a religious devotee. From this state he was saved by his mother Jijibai. She forced Tukaram by her entreaties to send her son back to the world on which he would have turned his back.

When Shivaji returned to his camp and his kingly duties, he did not lose touch with Tukaram. He often attended religious discourses given by Tukaram and his taste for them once nearly cost the king his life. Tukaram had at the king's request come to Poona and was reciting a *katha* or sacred story in the temple where Shiva used to worship, when a child. Some spy heard of this and told. A body of Afghans surrounded the temple and searched the audience. As the Afghans searched, a man, who in face and in clothes resembled Shivaji, ran through the door. The Afghans rushed after him, but never caught him. He disappeared in the forests of Sinhgad. In the meantime Tukaram continued his sacred story. When it was over, Shivaji and the rest of the audience went home unmolested. The belief still is widespread that the man who led the Afghans from the temple was none other than the god Krishna himself.

The main trend of Tukaram's poetry was a demand for true faith and not pretended goodness. It abounded in metaphors as the following verses show :

> 'A gold dish filled with milk pudding is put before a dog; a necklace of pearls is put round a donkey. Musk is smeared on a sow. A scholar preaches wisdom to a deaf man. What good comes of all this? Tuka says that only a saint knows the greatness of devotion.
>
> 'A frog sitting in a pool scorns the ocean. He has never seen the ocean and he wastes his breath in talking. A crow puffs himself out and claims to be better than a swan. An ass boasts that he is superior to an elephant. Tuka says that a gilt coin is not gold.'

The end of Tukaram has never been really cleared up. On one occasion the Brahmans, who disliked him, threw his writings into the Indrayani River, but they floated and were saved ; yet it was in the Indrayani that the poet himself perished. One day as he left home he told his wife Avalai that he was going to Vaikunth, the god Vishnu's heaven. He went to the banks of the Indrayani and, so it is believed, flung himself into the river either in a state of religious excitement or because he was suffering from some incurable disease. His followers believed and still believe that as Tukaram's spirit left his body, the chariot of the divine Ramachandra came down from heaven and bore Tukaram back into the skies (A.D. 1649). At any rate Tukaram never returned home again. He was deeply mourned not only by the unhappy Avalai, but by the whole countryside. And Dehu, his native village, is still a place of popular resort, to which every year the *varkaris* or pilgrims flock in thousands.

TEACHERS OF THE DECCAN

5. Ramdas

Ramdas was at once a product of the Pandharpur school and at the same time the first Deccan teacher definitely to break away from it. The Pandharpur saints overwhelmed by the servitude of their country, had preached resignation and devotion to the Lord Krishna. Ramdas lived in times, when the national feelings of Maharashtra had been stirred by the coming of a hero; and Ramdas' poetry no longer preached resignation, but a crusade against the oppressors of his fatherland.

Ramdas was a Deshasth Brahman and was born in A.D. 1608. He was the son of Suryaji, the village accountant of Jambgaon, in the Nasik District. His wife was one Ranubai and they were a pious and virtuous couple. For a long time their marriage was not blessed with any children; so both husband and wife prayed fervently to the Sun-god. In the end their prayers were answered and the Sun-god appeared to Ranubai in a vision. He promised her that she should have two sons. One of them would be an incarnation of himself, the Sun-god, and the other of Maruti, the Monkey-god who helped the divine hero Ramachandra. A year or two afterwards Ranubai gave birth to a son, whom she called Gangadhar and three years later to a second son, whom she called Narayan in honour of the Sun-god. Both the children were religiously inclined and when only five years old, Narayan, so it is said, had a vision of Maruti. Some years later, his parents decided to marry Narayan. He did not like the idea of marriage. After much pressure his mother got from him a promise that he would keep quiet until the ceremony, when the cloth separating the betrothed pair is withdrawn. She, no doubt, hoped that if Narayan stayed until this point was reached, he would feel it too late to go back. However, just before the verses that bind the marriage tie are pronounced, the priests called out '*Savadhan*' (Be on your guard), so as to warn the future householder that he is about to assume the cares and responsibilities of a householder. Narayan interpreted the word in a different sense. He ran from the room and hiding in a *pipal* tree, he escaped discovery for several days. His married life was thus ended before it began ; and leaving his parents, he wandered about the various holy places of India. Moropant in an admirable couplet has summed up the incident :

> 'At every marriage the Brahmans say, "*Savadhan*"; Ramdas (i.e., Narayan) alone obeyed them.'

In the course of his wanderings Narayan visited Benares, Ayodhya, Mathura and Prabhas. He went as far south as Rameshwaram, and so it is related, was carried by Maruti across the Palk Straits to see the virtuous king Bibhishan, placed on the throne of Lanka by the divine Ramachandra himself. From Ceylon Narayan went to Mahableshwar, where he stayed several months. He was very unwilling to visit Pandharpur ; for he did not wish to go to a spot, where the god Krishna had greater honour than his own beloved god Rama.

The god Krishna resolved, so it is said, to make the great saint visit his shrine. Taking the form of a Brahman, he met Narayan and pressed him to go to Pandharpur. Narayan refused because Krishna was honoured there more than Ramachandra. The Brahman said, 'But Maruti is honoured there more than either.' Narayan, who was believed to be an incarnation of Maruti, then decided to go there. When he reached Pandharpur, the god Maruti granted him a vision and told him that there was no difference between Ramachandra and Shri Krishna, since both were incarnations of Vishnu.

After his wanderings Narayan settled down at Chaphal in the Satara District. There he built a temple to Ramachandra and thinking that he had from birth been destined to the god's service, he changed his name from Narayan to Ramdas, or the 'slave of Rama'. The fame of the new saint spread over the Deccan and reached the ears of the great Shivaji. He was anxious to find a spiritual teacher in whose company he might turn from battle plans and statesmanship, to faith and devotion. He consulted the goddess Bhavani, who told the king to seek out Ramdas. For a long time Shivaji sought in vain; for the saint avoided him. At last he received a letter from Ramdas that pleased him greatly; but in it the saint expressed himself unwilling to be a courtier of the great king. The first verse ran as follows:

'O Meru of Resolution, O Helper of many, of unchanged resolve, rich and master of your passions! O Thou who pourest benefits on others, whose qualities are incomparable; Lord of men, horses and elephants! Lord of forts, earth and ocean! Leader and King who art strong always. King triumphant and famous, powerful and generous, meritorious, virtuous and wise. Possessed ever of conduct and judgment, generosity and faith, knowledge and character. Bold and generous, grave and daring, swift to execute. Thou, who by thy vigilance didst spurn kings. The holy places were broken. The abodes of Brahmans were polluted. All earth was shaken. Religion had fled. Narayan (the Sun-god) resolved to protect the gods of the faith, the cows, the Brahmans and inspired thee to do so.'

Shivaji liked the saint's letter so much that he went to Chaphal. Not finding Ramdas, he learnt from a female disciple that he had gone to Shringanwadi. She offered the king food, but he had vowed not to eat until he had found the saint. She gave him a guide and Shivaji found the saint writing under a tree. Ramdas blessed Shivaji, but would not go back with him. At the king's request, however, he gave Shivaji a letter on the art of government. The king offered Ramdas a sum of money but Ramdas distributed it among his cowherds. To Shivaji the saint gave as a parting gift a coconut, some water, some earth, a few pebbles and some horsedung. These Shivaji took to his mother. Jijabai asked scornfully the meaning of such a gift. Her son guessed easily the sage's meaning. The water and the earth meant that Shivaji would conquer Maharashtra. The pebbles meant that he would hold it by means of his fortresses. The horsedung meant that he would win his greatest successes by means of his cavalry.

Although Ramdas would not live in Shivaji's camp, the king induced him to settle at some place where he could easily be found. He gave Ramdas as a residence Parali, six miles from Satara and renamed it Sajjangad or 'the fort of a good man'.

One day the king met Ramdas at the ancient temple of Maruti on Jaranda Hill not very far from Satara. The saint asked for alms. Shivaji wrote some words on a piece of paper and dropped it into the sage's lap. Ramdas picked it up and read in it a grant of the entire kingdom. The saint affected to accept the grant and for the whole day, Shivaji, having no longer any property, acted as his servant. At the end of the day, Ramdas asked Shivaji how he liked the change from kingship to service. Shivaji replied that he was quite happy, provided that he was near his teacher. Ramdas gave back the grant and said, 'Take back your kingdom. It is for kings to rule and for Brahmans to pray.' Nevertheless Shivaji insisted that the saint should bestow on him his sandals, as Rama had done on his brother Bharata, so that the world might know that Ramdas and not Shivaji was the real king. He also chose for his flag the orange brown banner, which the pilgrims bear when they go to worship at Pandharpur. It is famous in history as the *Bhangwa Jhenda*. Ramdas outlived the great king by a single year and although he would not receive Sambhaji because of his cruelties, he wrote him an admirable letter begging him to model his rule on that of his father.

'Never forget,' he wrote, 'how Shivaji won his kingdom. If you call yourself a man try to do better than even he did.'

The last moments of Ramdas have been admirably described in Ramdas' life by Hanmant Swami. It was at Parali that the wise old Brahman felt his end approaching. His disciples felt it also and gave way to grief. Ramdas rebuked their tears and composed a few lines for them. Then he bade them read his poems and keep ever in their hearts the image of the god Ramachandra. A few moments later the dying saint called out 'Har! Har!' twenty-one times. He whispered the words 'Ram! Ram!' His eyes sought the god's image and a flame, so it seemed to the spectators, left his mouth and entered the lips of the image. His disciples called to him, but he made no answer. His body was burned to the north of Parali upon a pyre of *bel* and *tulsi* wood. His ashes were gathered and taken to Chaphal. Afterwards Sambhaji had them conveyed northwards and cast reverently into the Ganges River.

TEACHERS OF THE DECCAN

6. Mahipati

This charming poet deserves to be called a teacher of India, not because of any new doctrines that he preached, but because he was the biographer of the saints of Maharashtra. Without Mahipati's works we should know very little indeed of the poets of Pandharpur.

Mahipati was a Rigvedi Deshasth Brahman and was born in A.D 1715 in the village of Taharabad, some forty miles from Ahmadnagar. His father Dadopant, surnamed Kamble had according to tradition, served in the Moghul army. This is not improbable as Ahmadnagar was for many years later in the possession of the Moghuls. At the age of forty Dadopant resigned the Moghul service and returned to his village, where he had inherited the post of village accountant. He passed his remaining years as a pious and orthodox Brahman, making every month a pilgrimage to Pandharpur. Unfortunately he and his wife Ganga were childless and this was a cause of great sorrow to them both.

One day when Dadopant was at Pandharpur, he fell into a fit of despair. He reflected that all his devotion to the god Krishna had been useless, in that he would leave no son to make pilgrimages when he himself became too old to do so. That night he saw in a dream the god Krishna or Vithoba. The god stood by him and putting a ball of sweetmeats in his hand, told him to give it to his wife to eat. When Dadopant woke up, he was still holding a ball of sweetmeats. Convinced that it was a gift of the god, he took it home. His wife ate it and in less than a year she bore to her lord a son, the poet Mahipati.

Legend has it that from his earliest years Mahipaṭi showed signs of devotion and that seeing his father strike cymbals in honour of the god Krishna, the child used to imitate him by striking pebbles together. When Mahipati was five years old, his father whose health was failing, could no longer make his annual pilgrimages to Pandharpur. Mahipati begged to be sent instead and in the care of some pious *kasars* or makers of glass bangles, the little boy went on his first pilgrimage to the holy city.

Dadopant lived until Mahipati was sixteen, when he died leaving the office and lands of village accountant to his only son. The village, however, was part of the *jaghir* of a Musulman noble and to him Mahipati was responsible for the collection of the revenue. One day Mahipati had been, as usual, to the house of his Musulman master and on his return devoted himself to worship and prayer. A messenger came from the noble demanding Mahipati's immediate attendance. Mahipati told the messenger that he would attend on his master, when he had finished his duties to his god. This did not satisfy the Musulman, who sent an even more peremptory message. Mahipati left his prayers and went to his master's house. At the same time he felt that he could no longer serve both God and Mammon. Next day he took his pen and laid it before the image of Krishna and exclaimed, 'I can no longer serve two masters. Lord Krishna, thou art my true master. In Thy service I shall spend the remaining years of my life.' He then resigned the office of village accountant and never again entered service. This rule of independence has, so it is said, been faithfully kept by Mahipati's descendants to the present day. They still decline to accept appointments, even under the British Government.

After leaving his work as village accountant, Mahipati devoted himself wholly to prayers and vigils. One night, when exhausted by his penances, he had fallen asleep, he saw in a dream the poet Tukaram. The latter told him how he (Tukaram) had continued Namdev's work and how he and other saints had laboured for the love of the god Krishna. Let Mahipati now tell the story of the saints to the whole world. When Mahipati awoke he began the famous Bhaktavijaya. In it are told in verse simple, but full of the most delightful imagery, the lives of the various saints of Pandharpur from Dnyandev onwards. Mahipati wrote other works of a similar nature, *viz.*, the Kathesaramrit, the Santlilamrit, the Bhaktalilamrit and the unfinished Santvijaya. The latter contains a detailed account of the life of Ramdas.

Mahipati proved by his conduct that his saintliness was not a mere pretence. Once a famine raged in the Deccan and hundreds died of hunger. Mahipati, although himself a poor man, threw open the doors of his house and called in the starving beggars to take away what they could. A local landowner heard of Mahipati's generosity and sent the poet several carts full of grain; but these also Mahipati devoted to the relief of the hungry. When the famine had abated, Mahipati made it his rule to open wide the doors of his house once every third year, so that the poor might take away its contents. After some years his relatives begged him not to do so any more, as the custom might be held binding on his children. Mahipati agreed; but he built instead a small temple to the god Krishna and once a year he fed at its door the poor and the needy.

Mahipati died at the age of seventy-five in the year A.D. 1790. He left two sons Vithalboa and Narayanboa. The former became a well-known musician at the court of the luxurious Bajirao II and was a friend of Moropant, the father of modern Marathi poetry. Moropant greatly admired Mahipati and in a poem of fourteen stanzas, he gave the work of Mahipati the highest praise. 'May this praise be not hateful to Mahipati,' wrote Moropant. 'As a drop of oil spreads over the surface of a crystal lake, so the fame of the Bhaktavijaya has spread everywhere.' Moropant spoke no more than the truth for there are few poets more popular to-day in the Deccan than the graceful and musical Mahipati.

A TEACHER OF NORTHERN INDIA

7. KABIR

THERE is some doubt as to the date of Kabir's birth. According to Mr. R. Tagore, he was born about A.D. 1440. According to Mr. Macauliffe, Kabir was born in A.D. 1398. One story runs that Kabir was the son of a Brahman widow, who exposed him on the Lahar Lake. Acording to the Marathi poet Mahipati, Kabir was the reincarnation of the rishi Shuk and was not born of woman at all. A Musulman weaver was washing some thread in the Ganges, when he heard the cry of 'Ram ! Ram !' He looked up and saw a shell floating by. He picked up the shell, opened it and found inside a beautiful baby boy. The weaver, whose name has been variously given as Tamalmomin, Ali and Niru, took the child home and gave it to his wife Nima. Although not a mother, she was able miraculously to nurse it herself. As the weaver was a Musulman, he brought up the child as a Musulman and gave it the name of Kabir or the great one.

Benares is the centre of Hindu influences and the little boy was deeply affected by them. He often spent his time meditating on the hero-god Ramachandra, to the detriment of the weaving which he had been given to do. It is said that the god Krishna would at times work also at the loom and so save Kabir from the punishment which his idleness would otherwise have brought on him. Another story told by Mahipati runs as follows :—

When Kabir grew up, he married. His wife bore him a son, Kamal. Fifteen years or so later, a band of pilgrims came to visit Kabir. There was, however, no food in the house. Kabir and Kamal, sooner than send the holy men away hungry, went to a grocer's shop and with a crowbar made a hole in the wall. Kamal went inside and passed out through the hole grain and rice, molasses and vegetables. The grocer woke up and caught Kamal by the legs, as he was trying to wriggle back through the hole. Kabir to prevent discovery and at the boy's own wish cut Kamal's head off. Then he went home with the food and gave the pilgrims an excellent dinner. Next day the grocer took Kamal's headless body to the king, who had it impaled ; but at night Kabir took down the body, put back the head and Kamal once more came to life.

Ramanand was the great Hindu teacher of the time and Kabir wished to become his pupil. Kabir thought to himself, 'He who has no spiritual teacher is like a lifeless corpse or a childless house or a partridge on a moonless night.' Ramanand refused to take Kabir as a pupil, because he was a Musulman. Kabir dug a hole near Ramanand's hermitage and hid in it. Before dawn Ramanand went to bathe in the Ganges. As he went, he stumbled over Kabir and cried 'Ram ! Ram !'. Kabir sprang up and declared that Ramanand had accepted him as his pupil. After some hesitation Ramanand did so. There were many who objected to this Musulman-Hindu saint and to pay him out, his enemies sent letters to all the anchorites of India—to Hardwar,

Mathura, Vrindavan, Gokula and Dwarka, inviting them to visit Kabir. A great multitude appeared without any warning before Kabir's door. He had no food to give them, yet he dared not send away the anchorites for fear of incurring their anger. Again the god Krishna came to his help. Just as he had multiplied himself when dancing with the milkmaids of Gokula, so he multiplied himself into a thousand Kabirs. He created vast quantities of food and in this way not only gave the anchorites an excellent meal, but also waited on them and attended to their every wish. 'Thus,' wrote Mahipati, 'he satisfied the wants of every saint, just as in every pot you will find the sun's reflection.'

The Brahmans and Musulmans were alike scandalized at Kabir and complained to the emperor Sikandar Khan Lodi. He sent for Kabir, and grew angry when the latter refused to salute him. Kabir explained that he had no business with the emperor and that he reserved his salutes for the One God. The emperor loaded the saint with chains and threw him into the river. In the water the chains fell off and Kabir swam ashore. He was then thrown into a fiery furnace, but the fire went out and Kabir emerged uninjured. Lastly he was trussed up with ropes and a raging elephant was let loose at him; but the elephant was no match for the great teacher and ran away. The incident was described by Kabir in the following verses :—

> 'They tied my arms and threw me like a ball
> 'They beat an infuriated elephant on the head that he might trample on me.
> 'But he trumpeted and fled, saying,
> ' "I am a sacrifice to that shape which appeared." '

Kabir's enemies having failed to destroy his body by violence, tried to ruin his soul. They sent a beautiful courtesan to woo him ; but it was all in vain. The lovely girl found herself powerless to seduce the saint. In the end she yielded to his teaching and was converted like Magdalen to a holy life. As Kabir grew old, men let him alone. He wrote a vast collection of hymns, the object of which was to join together Hinduism and Islam. A beautiful selection of these hymns has been admirably translated by Mr. Rabindranath Tagore. The following lines embody Kabir's creed :—

> 'O Servant, where dost thou seek me?
> 'Lo! I am beside thee.
> 'I am neither in temple nor in mosque.
> 'I am neither in Kaaba nor in Kailas.
> 'Neither am I in rites nor in ceremonies;
> 'Nor in Yoga nor in renunciation.
> 'If thou art a true seeker, thou shalt at once see Me, thou shalt meet Me in a moment of time.
> 'Kabir says "O Sadhu! God is the breath of all breath." '

Kabir lived to an immense age, no less than 119½ years. Up to his last year, he lived at Benares. Then he migrated to Magahar to die. The reason was that according to the Brahmans, if a man died at Magahar, he could not possibly be happy in his next existence. To disprove this, Kabir went to Magahar beyond the Ganges. He died there and since his death, *Kabirpanthis* or followers of Kabir say that Magahar is the holiest of all places. Before his death Kabir wrote :

> 'For many years I did penance at Benares
> 'I consider Magahar as good as Benares
> 'How shall he of scant devotion be saved?'

After Kabir's death, Hindus and Musulmans quarrelled over the disposal of his corpse. The Rajput Raja of Benares wanted to burn it, while Bijli Khan, the Nawab of Gorakhpur, wished to bury it. At last a voice from the skies forbade the quarrel. When the combatants looked for the corpse, it had vanished. A heap of scented flowers lay in its place. The Musulmans made a grave and buried in it some of the flowers. The Hindus built a temple where the other flowers had lain. Let us trust that when Kabir died he was as he wished, united to his beloved, the Lord Krishna:

'How could the love between Thee and me sever?
'As the leaf of the lotus abides on the water: so Thou art my Lord and I am Thy servant.
'As the nightbird chakor gazes all night at the moon: so Thou art my Lord and I am Thy servant.
'From the beginning until the ending of time there is love between Thee and me; and how shall such love be extinguished.
'Kabir says "As the river enters the Ocean, so my heart touches Thee." '

TEACHERS OF GUZARAT

8. Mirabai[1]

Of all India's teachers there is none with a more romantic history than Mirabai. Her doings have been sung by Mahipati. She has found a place in Tod's Rajasthan ; and selections from her works are to be found in every collection of Indian poems. Beautiful and accomplished, highly born and daring, she was one of the few who having great possessions are yet willing to give them up for their faith.

Mahipati describes Mirabai as a daughter of Udaipur. Colonel Tod more correctly speaks of her as a princess of Jodhpur but as the queen of Kumbho Rana, who succeeded to the throne of Udaipur in A.D. 1491. According to Mr. Mehta, who follows Deviprasad and Kavi Samaldas, she was the daughter of Ratansingh and the grand-daughter of Dudaji Rana of Jodhpur. According to Mr. Mehta she was born about A.D. 1499. According to Mr. Jhaveri she was born in A.D. 1403. She lost her mother when a child ; and thereafter she was in the care of her grandfather Rana Dudaji, who was an ardent devotee of the Lord Krishna. One day Mirabai watched a marriage procession go by the palace at Jodhpur. She got childishly excited and plied her grandfather with questions about her own marriage and her future husband. At last the Rana,

[1]*Mirabai*, a Guzarati work, by W. B. B. N. Mehta (M. C. Kathari, Baroda).

weary of her chatter, said, 'Your husband will be the Lord Krishna.' Unhappily the words spoken in jest were taken seriously by the little maid. She vowed that the Lord Krishna and none other should be her husband. One day a Sadhu or anchorite came to the palace, bearing with him an image of the god. The little princess begged it of him but he refused to give it. To get her way, she fasted and prayed continuously. At last the Lord Krishna appeared in a vision to the Sadhu and bade him give her the image. All her life she kept it and deemed it her greatest treasure.

In spite of her vow to wed the Lord Krishna, the time came when Rana Dudaji had to find Mirabai an earthly husband. He chose for her Bhojraj, the heir to the noblest throne in India, that of Udaipur or as it then was Chitor. Her married life was short and unhappy and the young prince died soon after her marriage. Having lost her husband, her thoughts turned back to religion and she scandalized the great house into which she had married by mixing always with religious ascetics and anchorites. Her father-in-law Rana Sangramsingh, died soon after Prince Bhojraj and her brother-in-law Rana Ratansing, at the prompting of his mother, shut Mirabai up in a place, haunted by man-slaying *bhuts* or ghosts. It was in vain ; for the *bhuts* fled in terror at the Lord Krishna's name and never returned. It was then resolved to poison her. The Rana sent her a bowl of poison with a message that it was a bowl of ambrosia. Mirabai showed it first to the image of Krishna and then drank it. The poison did the princess no harm ; but the idol turned from black to a hideous green. The Rana then sent several ladies of his family to lead her from the course that she had set herself; but instead of changing her, they were themselves converted and became ardent worshippers of Shri Krishna. At last the Rana went to Mirabai's living rooms, resolved to rid himself of the troublesome widowed princess. When he tried to cut her down he saw four Mirabais in front of him and could not hit the real one. After he had missed her several times, the Lord Krishna appeared in the guise of Nar Sinh the man-lion that tore in pieces the wicked Hiranyakasipu. Brave Rajput although he was, the Rana fled in terror before the awful apparition.

There was but one thing left and that was to send Mirabai back to Jodhpur. Unhappily Mirabai's ways were no more pleasing to her Rahtor kinsmen than they had been to the prince of Chitor. After a short stay at Jodhpur, she left it on a pilgrimage to Vrindavan. There she met an anchorite named Gosainyogi, who journeyed with her to Benares and thence to Dwarka. At Dwarka she dwelt for the rest of her life. It was there that she achieved what has been often said to be impossible. She wrote poetry of the first order in a foreign tongue. The following is a translation of one of her poems made by Mr. Jhaveri, Chief Judge of the Small Cause Court of Bombay[1] and reproduced with some slight changes by his kind permission. In the poem Mirabai describes her hatred of the Rana and her flight from Chitor:

'Govind (Krishna) is my Lord and for all else I feel dislike. I adore my Ramji (Ramachandra), none other

[1] See *Milestones in Guzarati Literature*, by Mr. Jhaveri—a book of the highest merit.

is worth anything in my eyes. In the palace of Mirabai live those (the Sadhus) who love Hari (Krishna). Hari lives far from the falsehearted; but he lives close to my Sadhus. The Rana sends Mirabai a letter and bids her give up their company and live with him. Mirabai answers him and bids him resign his throne and live with them. The Rana sent a cup full of poison for Mirabai and she drank it, deeming it nectar. The Lord of the World helped her. O camelman! make ready your camel, I have hundreds of miles to travel. I think it a sin even to drink water in the lands of the Rana. Mira kept Mewar to her left and rode towards the west. She left her all because she loved not Maya.'

The end of Mira was tragic, but it was a fitting end for one who loved more than her life the service of the Lord Krishna. After Mirabai had left Chitor the Rana fell upon evil days. The Delhi emperors laid a heavy hand on Rajputana and the Sisodias only kept their freedom by dint of ceaseless and wearing effort. In his despair the Rana thought of Mirabai. If he could beg her pardon and win the saintly princess back to Chitor, all might be well. At first she refused to the great joy of Dwarka, for her fame as a saint had become the glory of all Kathiawar. Again and again the Rana sent messages couched in humbler and humbler terms. At last Mirabai felt that she could refuse no longer. With breaking heart she went into the great temple to bid a last good-bye to her beloved god. When she had finished speaking, she held out her arms to embrace the image. The arms of the image stretched out to meet hers and as the god clasped to his bosom the beautiful princess, her spirit left her body and was united with His for ever.

TEACHERS OF GUZARAT

9. NARSINH MEHTA

NARSINH MEHTA has been styled the Chaucer of Guzarat; but the name hardly does him justice. Few except scholars read Chaucer's nowadays in England, whereas Narsinh Mehta's hymns are every morning sung or hummed by hundreds of men and women all over Kathiawar and Guzarat.

Narsinh Mehta was a Nagar Brahman of Junagadh in Kathiawar but according to the Marathi poet Mahipati, he had a previous existence as a tiger. The poet's whimsical tale runs as follows :—

One day the god Shiva was looking at a tiger's skin and as he looked at it, his spirit passed into the body of a live tiger. Now it so happened that King Pipaji, a very saintly king of Gademandal, had been with his queen to Benares to learn true devotion from the sage Ramanand. On their return journey, the king and queen had to pass through a forest. There they met the very tiger into whose body Shiva's spirit had entered. It was about to spring on them, when King Pipaji, from whom perfect love of the Lord Krishna had cast out all fear, went up to it. He put his hand on its head and said, 'From henceforth worship the Lord Krishna night and day.' The raging beast fell at the king's feet and begged for pardon. The king soothed it and putting a *tulsi* garland round its neck, taught it to repeat the names of the Lord Krishna. King Pipaji and his queen went their way until they reached Gademandal. The tiger repenting of its sins, gave up taking life and roamed about the forest, singing the praises of the Lord Krishna. This it did for seven days, growing gradually weaker and weaker. At last it died repeating the great god's name. As a reward for its piety it was born again as Narsinh Mehta.

His next birth was in A.D. 1414 (St. 1470) in the small village of Talaja near Junagadh. His father was a Nagar Brahman called Krishnamodar. His mother's name was Dyakor. He had two elder brothers Jivanram and Narbharam. Krishnamodar died when his son Narsinh was only three and the penniless family had to take refuge with his uncle Parbatdas.

One tale has it that Narsinh Mehta was dumb until he was eight. One day a wandering Bawa or minstrel put his hand on the child's head and said, 'Speak the words, Shri, Radha, Krishna.' The boy's dumbness left him for ever and he spoke the three sacred words without difficulty. Yet even though Narsinh Mehta ceased to be dumb, he remained dull and stupid; and the family into which he should have married, broke off the match because he was so backward. This disaster so affected Narsinh's mother Dyakor, that she died of a broken heart. When Narsinh was seventeen, he did secure a wife, a girl called Manekbai from the distant village of Una. Not long after Narsinh's marriage Parbatdas died, leaving the boy dependent on his brothers, who had now grown to manhood. They resented the burden, especially as Narsinh, already inclined to devotion, spent all his time with religious singers. Another cause of offence was that, whereas all the Nagar community were strict followers of the god Shiva, Narsinh was a fervent devotee of the Lord Krishna. At last Narsinh's brother's wife could keep her temper no longer. She said to him, 'A washerman's stone slab is more useful than you are!' This was too much for Narsinh. He left his brother's house and fled to Gopnath on the sea-coast of Kathiawar. There he fasted and prayed to the god Shiva, his family god, until at last the mighty deity took pity on him. On the seventh day of the penance Shiva appeared to Narsinh in all his splendour and glory. He bade Narsinh ask for a boon. Narsinh asked falteringly for a vision of the Lord Krishna. Shiva granted it and dressing the boy as a milkmaid, bore him away to Dwarka, where the fortunate youth was allowed to see the dance of the Lord Krishna with the *gopis*. The vision determined Narsinh's career and from a backward boy he became a deeply inspired poet. His first couplet was in praise of his brother's wife who by her cruel speech had been the instrument to win him a vision of the Lord Krishna :

> 'Praise be to my brother's wife! She spoke harshly to me.
> 'Then I, Narsinh, lost all fear and saw Krishna, Life of the World.'

Narsinh, with his wife and children soon afterwards left his brother's house and lived in a little hut, where now is to be seen the platform known as Narsinh's Choro ; but he was as sore a trial to his wife Manekbai as afterwards Tukaram proved to Avalai. He earned no money, but spent his days in devotional songs and dances. His wife scolded and railed at him. but he replied in a well-known line :—

> 'Eva amc re eva re eva, tame kaho cho wali teva re.'
> I was like this always and shall be whatever you say.

The time, however, came when he had to find a husband for his daughter Kuvarbai and he had no dowry to give her. However, just as the Lord Krishna helped Kabir and Tukaram, so he helped Narsinh Mehta. He took the form of his disciple and offered with Kuvarbai so rich a dower of diamonds, precious stones and costly raiment, that she had no difficulty in finding a husband.

Not long after Kuvarbai's marriage, his wife Manekbai died and her death was followed by that of their remaining children. Kuvarbai had gone to her husband's house; so Narsinh, after the first agony of grief had passed away, rejoiced rather than sorrowed in his freedom from worldly ties :—

> 'It is well; my anxieties have passed. Now I shall worship Shri Gopal (Krishna) at my ease.'

Narsinh denounced caste restrictions, provided the low caste were devotees of Krishna. For consorting with Dheds and worshipping Krishna rather than Shiva, Narsinh was persecuted by the Nagars and by the ruler of Junagadh, Ra Mandlik. The Nagars excluded Narsinh from their caste dinners; but they were punished by the appearance at the next caste dinner of a Dhed between every pair of Nagars. Nor could they rid themselves of the unwelcome guests, until they had craved Narsinh's pardon and begged him to join them. The punishment reserved for Ra Mandlik was more severe. Junagadh was conquered by the Musulmans. He himself had to pay a humiliating tribute and only kept his throne by embracing Islam.

Narsinh Mehta lived to the age of sixty-six. Shortly before his death, he was in great pain; but he had vowed to write 125,000 Padas or hymns. He had only written 100,000 and his soul would not leave his body because of the unwritten 25,000. His daughter-in-law, the widow of his dead son, found him in this unhappy state. She promised to write in his stead the remaining 25,000 hymns. Satisfied with this promise, Narsinh's soul was at last set free. Fortified by the dead man's spirit, the young widow was able to keep her promise and she wrote the unwritten Padas.

GURU NANAK

TEACHERS OF THE PUNJAB

10. GURU NANAK

THE first thing that strikes a visitor to Sind from the Deccan, after he has absorbed the difference in the physical geography, is the gulf between the Hindus of Sind and the Hindus of Maharashtra. There was an old Greek proverb that said, '*Sophias arche, kuriou phobos*' or the fear of one's lord is the beginning of wisdom. That may have worked well in Hellas, but in India independent enquiries will prove more valuable. If my visitor then begins to probe the matter, he will find that the bulk of the so called Hindus are not orthodox worshippers of the Hindu Triad, but disciples of Nanak Shah. The next stage of enquiry is for the visitor to find out who was Nanak Shah; and in this chapter I propose to save him further trouble by giving a short sketch of that much-revered spiritual leader.

In the month of November,[1] A.D. 1469, Nanak was born in Talwandi in the modern district of Lahore. His parents were Kalu the village accountant and Tripta his wife. Like Zoroaster, Nanak is said to have been born laughing or, to use his mother's phrase, his first cry was, 'as the laughing voice of a wise man joining a social gathering.' Many tales are told of his precocious

[1] The date is disputed. Another tradition has it that Nanak was born in Vaishakh (April-May).

intelligence, but although he was so quick to absorb knowledge, he soon abandoned worldly studies, telling his school-master, 'To your accomplishments I prefer the study of divine knowledge.' He then, like many another religious reformer, betook himself to the woods and listened to the teachings of the sages and anchorites, who had sought shelter there from religious persecution. From them he learnt a great deal; and at fourteen his education was far wider than that of other boys of his age. It was, however, time for him to marry and he married Sulakhani, the daughter of one Mula, a resident of Batala in the Gurdaspur District. She bore him in due course two sons, Shri Chand and Lakshmidas.

His father Kalu was anxious to see his son settled in life and after great difficulty persuaded him to become a shopkeeper. He gave Nanak money with which to buy, at the neighbouring town of Chuharkhana, stock for his shop. On the way Nanak met some starving anchorites and spent the money in feeding them. When he returned home without either money or purchases, his exasperated father boxed his ears. Nanak smarting at his father's treatment, left the family house. For a short time he was storekeeper to the governor of Sultanpur; then he became a fakir and began his interminable wanderings. With him journeyed a disciple called Mardana, a Musulman Dum or hereditary minstrel. In the course of his travels Nanak met a notorious robber called Shaikh Sajjan. This ingenious person had built, to attract wayfarers, both a Hindu temple and a mosque; and he had the manners and tact of an ambassador. Unhappily his subsequent conduct belied his victims' first impressions. Once his guests had gone to sleep, he murdered and robbed them and threw their bodies into a neighbouring well. But it was useless for Sheikh Sajjan to try to trick the divine intelligence of Nanak. With the speed of thought, his wickedness was unmasked and he himself converted. He was forced to distribute among the poor his stolen wealth and became a religious ascetic.

There is no doubt but that Nanak was deeply influenced by Islam. He never, it is true, became a Musulman or anything approaching one; for he never accepted Mohomed as a prophet. But he preached monotheism. His doctrine is summarized in the preamble to the Japji.

> 'There is but one God whose name is true, the Creator devoid of fear and enmity, immortal, unborn, self-existent, great and bountiful. Repeat his name.
>
> 'The True one was in the beginning; the True one was in the primal age;
>
> 'The True one, is, was, O Nanak; the True one also shall be.'

He condemned the idols of orthodox Hinduism with great vigour especially at Vrindavan, Mathura and Puri; and after wandering through India, Afghanistan and Ceylon, he resolved to go to Mecca. This was a most daring thing to do, although not perhaps so dangerous then as now. He dressed adequately for the part in the blue garb of a Musulman pilgrim. He carried a staff, a cup for his ablutions and a praying carpet. The faithful Mardana shared the perils of the high adventure. On the way they passed a night pleasantly with a Musulman fakir; but next day the fakir took fright, because a cloud just over Nanak's head kept pace with them. He bade Nanak and Mardana leave him and walked on alone.

In due course Nanak and Mardana reached Mecca. Their ignorance of local customs soon got them into trouble. Tired with the journey, Nanak went to sleep with his feet towards the holy Kaaba, for which he cared not at all. An Arab priest deeply shocked, kicked him violently and asked him why he slept with his feet turned towards God. Nanak answered, 'Put my feet where God is not.' The priest seized Nanak by the legs and swung him round. As he swung in a circle, the holiest of all mosques followed his feet, until completing the circle, it returned to its starting place. This striking miracle attracted the priests from all Mecca. They questioned him concerning the nature of God. His reply shows how far removed he was both from Islam and Hinduism. I quote the following lines only :—

> 'How great shall I call God? to whom shall I go regarding him?
>
> 'He is the greatest of the great and great is his world; men depart in their pride.
>
> 'I have consulted the four Vedas, but their writings find not God's limits.
>
> 'I have consulted the four books of the Musulman's, but God's work is not described in them.
>
> 'I, Nanak, say that man shall be true to his faith, if he fear God and do good works.'

From Mecca Nanak moved to Medina and from Medina to Baghdad. There he shouted the call to prayer with great vehemence, but substituted words of his own for the words *Mahomed al rasul Allah* (Mahomed is the prophet of God). Nanak's apparent fervour drew the attention of the high priest of Baghdad, who asked him to what sect he belonged. Nanak replied,

> 'I have appeared in this age to indicate the way unto men. I reject all sects and only know one God, whom I recognize in the earth, the heavens and in all directions.'

The high priest was enraged at what he deemed heresy and would have laid hands on 'the very impious fakir.' Nanak however managed to escape and returned to India through the Persian Gulf. After a short stay in Multan, he and Mardana settled at Kartarpur.

There the faithful Mardana fell ill and died. He had been a Musulman, so the question arose as to the disposal of his body. Nanak held that as Mardana had become a Sikh (or one divinely learned) and knew God, he had become the equal of a Brahman ; thus on Mardana's death his body was consigned to the River Ravi.

On the death of his old henchman, Nanak appointed his son Shahzada to act as minstrel in his father's place ; but the shock of Mardana's death proved too much for Nanak. He did not long survive his friend and disciple. Among the more intimate associates of his later years was one Lahina, a converted priest of Durga. To him Nanak, on feeling his end come near, gave his spiritual succession, naming him Angad or 'Produced from my body'. He passed over his two sons, who had rebelled against him and placed the umbrella of spiritual sovereignty over the head of Angad and bowed down before him. Before Nanak's death a quarrel arose between his Hindu and Musulman followers (for he had attracted numerous disciples from Islam) as to the disposal of his corpse. The former wished to burn, the latter to bury it. Nanak was asked to decide. He said, 'Let the Hindus place flowers on my right and the Musulmans on my left. They whose flowers are found fresh to-morrow morning may have the disposal of my body.' After the flowers had been put on each side of him, the prophet drew his sheet over the flowers as well as himself. Next morning the sheet was found unchanged. The disciples removed it, thinking to find the saint's dead body beneath it. The flowers would then guide them as to its disposal. Both sets of flowers they found equally fresh and blooming; but the body had wholly disappeared. The time of Nanak's departure from the earth was on some date in September, A.D. 1538 and it happened at Kartarpur.

The sayings of the great saint were the first to be recorded in the *Granth Sahib*, the holy book of the Sikhs. His verses were very numerous and are worthy of attention; I quote at random the following verses addressed to the all too bibulous Mardana.

> 'The barmaid is misery, wine is lust; man is the drinker.
>
> 'The company is false and covetous and it is ruined by excess of drink.
>
> 'Instead of such wine make good conduct thy yeast, truth thy molasses, God's name thy wine.
>
> 'Make merits thy cakes, good conduct thy clarified butter and modesty thy meat to eat.
>
> 'Such things, O Nanak, are obtained by the guru's favour; by partaking of them sins depart.'

TEACHERS OF THE PUNJAB

11. Guru Angad

I have mentioned in my previous chapter that Nanak appointed as his successor, a faithful disciple named Lahina, to whom he gave the name of Angad. Lahina was the son of a trader called Pheru, who had a shop in Matte di Serai, a village in the Firozpur District of the Punjab. Lahina's early life was uneventful. He married a lady called Khivi, a resident of his own village and by her he had a daughter Amro and two sons Dasu and Datu. When Matte di Serai was sacked by Mughals and Baluchis, Pheru and Lahina fled with their families to Khadur in the Amritsar District. Lahina had become a devout Hindu and had organized pilgrimages to Jwalamukhi in honour of the goddess Durga; but one day he heard a Sikh of Khadur, named Jodha, sing some lines of Nanak Shah:

> 'Ever remember that Lord by worshipping whom thou shalt find happiness.
> 'Do absolutely nothing evil: look well before thee.
> 'So throw the dice, that thou mayest not lose with the Lord.
> 'Nay, that thou mayest gain some profit.'

The effect of the song was magical. Lahina's heart was filled with religious feeling. He had no peace until he had learnt from Jodha who the author was. Having learnt that he was Jodha's Guru

Nanak, Lahina longed to behold Nanak 'as the mountain partridge longs to see the moon.'

Lahina was at this time about to start on a pilgrimage, but he induced the other pilgrims to go with him to Kartarpur. There he met Guru Nanak and lost all desire to worship Durga. His companions left him behind in disgust; but he resolved to become the body servant of Nanak. He first went home to tell his wife his intention and then returned to Kartarpur. When he did so, he found the Guru in his fields, unable to transport three bundles of grass to his cows at home. The grass was wet and muddy and the Sikhs with him refused to carry them; so, too, did his sons Sri Chand and Lakshmidas. They pleaded that to carry bundles was a cooly's work. Just then Lahina came up. Lifting on his head all three bundles, although one was a man's load, he carried them all dripping to Nanak's home. When they reached it, Nanak's wife reproached him for letting a visitor spoil his clothes by carrying muddy bundles; but the Guru replied, 'This is not mud; it is saffron of God's court, which marketh the elect.' As Nanak spoke, the mud on Lahina's clothes turned to saffron. The three bundles are to-day deemed by pious Sikhs to symbolize spiritual affairs, temporal affairs and the guruship.

After Lahina had become Guru, he adopted the name of Angad conferred on him, as I have said, by Nanak and was known by no other. Some years later the emperor Humayun, driven by Sher Shah from Bengal to Hindustan came to Lahore in the hope of finding a 'wonder working' priest, who would get him back his dominion. He heard of Guru Angad and went to Khadur, to which place the saint had returned. The emperor went laden with presents, for he thereby hoped to win Angad's favour. Angad was at the time in a deep trance, surrounded by minstrels who played and choristers who sang Nanak's hymns. The emperor had to wait and grew very angry. He put his hand on his sword hilt, wishing to draw his sword and cut down the saint. The sword, however, would not leave its scabbard and Angad said to him severely, 'When thou oughtest to have used thy sword against Sher Shah, thou didst not. Now when thou comest among priests, thou wishest to draw thy sword on them, instead of saluting them respectfully.' The emperor recovered his temper and apologized. The Guru answered, 'Hadst thou not put thy hand on thy sword hilt, thou shouldst at once have got back thy kingdom. Now thou must go to Persia; but when thou returnest, thou shalt recover thy possessions.' The prophecy was fulfilled. Humayun was driven out of India, but on Sher Shah's death he returned and recovered his empire.

Of the many stories told about Angad, this one has always pleased me most. A certain Sikh called Mana, worked as Angad's cook. Through excess of good living, he grew fat and proud. He quarrelled with his fellow-servants and the mere thought of work made him tremble all over. At last the Guru got tired of him and told him to go into the forest and cremate himself. Mana started off full of zeal. He gathered wood, set fire to it and watched it blaze; but the more the fire blazed, the less Mana liked the idea of jumping into it. Just then a thief came up, who asked him what he was doing. Mana told him his story; and as he did so, he spoke warmly of the virtues of the Guru, of whom he was genuinely fond. The thief was touched by Mana's eloquence and repented. He gave Mana a casket of jewels that he had stolen, and trusting Mana's assurance that he would thereby win salvation, he took Mana's place and leapt into the fire. When the thief's body had been well and truly burned, Mana went into the bazaar and tried to sell the jewels. He was arrested on suspicion. The owner of the jewels was traced and they were restored to him. The unhappy Mana was hanged. When the Guru heard of Mana's untimely end, he observed :

> 'So true it is, that perverse lose both worlds, and if Folly leave not the heart, man obtaineth not salvation even by living near the Guru.'

In any case the Guru had rest from Mana, that fat and proud one !

Just as Nanak had preferred to his sons a disciple, so Angad chose Amardas as his successor rather than his own sons. Amardas is said to have been descended from Bharat, the younger brother of the divine hero Ramachandra ; his father was Tejbhan a Khattri of Basarka near Amritsar. Tejbhan's wife Bakht Kaur bore him four sons, of whom the eldest was Amardas, born in May, A.D. 1479. Amardas was a devout Vaishnava and used to fast every eleventh day. In spite of his piety, he was greatly concerned, because he had no spiritual teacher. 'How can the lotus bloom without the sight of the sun !' he would exclaim, 'and how can man obtain salvation without a guru !' Early one morning he heard Angad's daughter Amro singing a hymn of Nanak. Amardas was charmed with it and begged her to sing it over again. He then asked her to tell him where she learnt it. She replied that she had learnt it from her father. Amardas prevailed on Amro to take him to Khadur and present him to Angad. Angad welcomed him, converted him to the Sikh religion and accepted his devoted service.

One day a man called Gobind came to Angad and made a complaint. His grievance was that, during a lawsuit, he had vowed that if he won it, he would found a city in Angad's honour and call it after him. He won the lawsuit, obtained from the emperor a grant of land on the Bias River and began his building operations. His masons worked strenuously all day; but at night some malicious demons pulled down the rising walls and the city made no progress. Gobind begged Angad to drive away the demons and grant to the new town the honour of his name. The Guru at first said, 'Why trouble about miserable human affairs? There should be nothing dearer to man than the True Name.' Gobind, however, persuaded Angad to help him build the town, even if he would not give it his name. The Guru gave Amardas his walking stick and with it the latter drove away the demons and marked out the town. It was built without further demoniac opposition. Amardas gave it the name of Gobindwal in honour of the builder. It is now known as Goindwal.

Even as a firefly feels jealous of the sun, so a rancorous and evil-minded ascetic or Tapasi of Khadur felt the most unholy jealousy of Angad. One day the rains failed and famine threatened the villagers. They went to the Tapasi and called on him to help them. He replied that the famine had been sent to punish their sin in honouring a married guru like Angad, instead of reverencing wholeheartedly a true anchorite like himself. 'If you expel him from the town,' said the Tapasi, 'you shall have rain in twenty-four hours.' The villagers, excited by the Tapasi's promises, went to Angad and told him either to call down rain himself or to leave the town. When Angad refused to call down rain, they drove him forth from Khadur. The Tapasi was at first pleased at Angad's expulsion, but when the villagers called on him to fulfil his promise and bring rain, his satisfaction left him. For a time he put them off with vain promises. At last they lost all patience and at Amardas's instigation, they beat the Tapasi very severely and drove him out also. Then they brought Angad back to Khadur. The latter was too kindhearted to rejoice at the condign punishment meted out to the odious Tapasi. He rebuked Amardas in words remarkable for their wide and generous charity :—

> 'Thou shouldst bear pardon in thy heart and do good to everyone irrespective of his acts. Thou shouldst deem gold and dross as the same and practise humility, for the humble shall ever be exalted. The pearl is small, but consider its price. Think of the tiny fruit of the *bohr* tree,[1] yet to what a size it groweth, filling the whole forest.'

When Angad's life began to near its end, he sent for five copper coins and a coco-nut, bathed Amardas, clothed him and placed him in the Guru's seat. Angad put the five copper coins and the coco-nut before Amardas, while Bhai Budha, another favourite disciple, put on his forehead the *tilak* or mark of

[1] The *Ficus Indica*.

Guruship. On the day of Angad's death, he rose before dawn, bathed and put on a new raiment to prepare for his final departure. He said good-bye to his family and ordered Guru Amardas to live at Goindwal instead of at Khadur. He then fixed his thoughts on Nanak and with the word '*Wahguru*' on his lips passed from this transitory world. (April, A.D. 1552). His body was not committed to the river as Nanak's had been, but at Angad's expressed wish, it was burnt on a pyre of sandal wood.

TEACHERS OF THE PUNJAB

12. Guru Amardas

Amardas's succession to the guruship was not unopposed. After Angad's death, his son Datu tried to usurp his father's place. He sat on the Guru's seat at Khadur and issued the following proclamation :—

'Amru (Guru Amardas) is old. He is my servant. I am prince of the Guru's line. His throne is mine.'

The proclamation, however, did Datu no good. The Sikhs of Khadur left Khadur and joined their brethren at Goindwal, where Guru Amardas was living. Datu bore his rival's growing fame for some time ; but at last he could bear it no longer. Early one morning he went to Goindwal, where he saw Guru Amardas enthroned in splendour. In a fury Datu said to him, 'Only yesterday thou wert a water-carrier in our house and to-day thou sittest as a guru.' With these words he kicked the Guru off the throne and sat on it himself. The Guru replied meekly, 'O Great King, pardon me. Thou must have hurt thy foot !' With these words he fled from Goindwal to his native place Basarka. The Sikhs were shocked at Datu's conduct, but as Amardas had not told them whither he was going, they did not know where he had gone and were unable to comfort him. At last they took his mare with them and letting her loose, followed in her tracks. She led them straight to the Guru's house at Basarka. They would have opened the door, but they read with concern the following words written on it. 'Whoever openeth this door is no Sikh of mine, nor am I his guru.' They were not long at a loss. They made a hole in Amardas's wall and entered through the hole. The Guru was at first put out by their unceremonious entrance, but at last he smiled and forgave them.

In the meantime things had been going badly with the rebellious Datu. He had at first rejoiced in his usurpation of the Guru's throne; but afterwards he found that he had gained nothing thereby. The Sikhs would neither do him homage, nor give him offerings. In disgust he put on a camel all the wealth that he could find in Amardas's house and set out for Khadur. On the way he was attacked by robbers, who took all his illgotten gold. When he protested, one of them struck him with a lathi on the very foot that had kicked Guru Amardas; and it swelled up as big as a kettledrum and caused him frightful pain.

Guru Amardas was very anxious to do away with caste and the seclusion of women. Once the Raja of Haripur brought one of his queens to see the Guru. The latter, however, would not receive the Raja until he had eaten with other visitors in his kitchen regardless of caste. The Rani, however, would not take off her veil. The Guru said to her, 'Crazy lady, if thou art not pleased with the Guru's face, why hast thou come hither?' The poor queen instantly became really crazy. She tore off her clothes and ran naked into the forest. One day she met a half-witted servant of the Guru, whose habit of saying, 'Sach, Sach' had earned him the nickname of Sachansach. He was gathering firewood but the mad woman rushed at him and tore him all over with her nails. The wretched Sachansach went home in a sorry plight and wished to resign the Guru's service. When Amardas heard what had happened, he gave Sachansach his slipper and said, 'If the witch meets you again, touch her with this and she will be cured.' Sachansach next day went into the forest. The queen again met him and rushed at him. Sachansach touched her with the Guru's slipper and her reason returned. Then she saw to her horror that she was naked and tried to run away. Sachansach tore his single blanket in two and gave her half. In this wretched guise she again went to see the Guru and fell at his feet. He forgave her and sent her back to her lord, the Raja of Haripur.

A family that still reside at Goindwal and bear the name of Maipotre recall one of the most striking of the Guru's miracles. A goldsmith of Goindwal and his wife, both well stricken in years, were childless. As they wished greatly to have children, they began to dig a well and build a temple in the hope of acquiring merit and thereafter offspring. The Guru heard of their pious wish to dig a well and build a temple and went to see if he could help them. As soon as he came, the goldsmith and his wife threw themselves at the feet of the Guru and begged him for an heir. The Guru indignantly asked them whether they supposed that he kept children always with him to give to his friends. The goldsmith replied in all humility, 'There are children in the mere words of the Guru.' The Guru was pleased with the answer and said, 'In that you both have faith, you shall have two children.' The wife bore in due course two sons. She seemed, however, so old to be their mother, that the villagers called the boys 'Maipotre' or 'Mother's grandsons'; and their descendants are so called to this day.

Just as Angad had been tormented by a Tapasi, so another Tapasi or ascetic came to Goindwal to torment Amardas. This Tapasi's heart was as bitter as colocynth, but his words were as sweet as the mango. One day the Guru gave a great feast and invited the Tapasi. The latter refused the invitation and went instead to dine uninvited with the governor of the province. The Tapasi lost by the exchange; from the governor he got a bad dinner and only a rupee as a present. The Guru gave his guests an excellent meal and presents varying from five to sixteen rupees. The greedy Tapasi sent his son to get, if he could, his share of the Guru's dinner. Amardas very kindly gave him his father's portion as well as five rupees. The Tapasi however, continued to slander and blaspheme the Guru, but his curses came home to roost. His son while returning with his father's portion, broke his leg. The Tapasi, himself, died soon afterwards.

Amardas had two sons Mohan and Mohri and two daughters Dani and Bhani. Dani was married to one Rama of Guru Nanak's family, Bhani, who was given to religious meditation, was at first averse to the married state. She used to say to her playmates, 'We are but thoughtless beings. We skip and play about like lambs, yet all the while the butcher Death standeth over us.' Nevertheless her mother Mansa Devi pressed Amardas to find her a husband when Bhani reached puberty. One day a boy came to their door, hawking some articles. His beauty attracted Amardas and Mansa Devi. They both decided that he was the very husband for Bhani. After due enquiries she was betrothed to the boy and married. His name was Ramdas, but he was commonly called Jetha. Some years later the great Akbar on the way to Lahore, stopped to visit Goindwal and meet Amardas, of whose merits he had often heard. The Guru made no distinction between emperors and other men. Akbar had to eat in Amardas's kitchen of coarse rice before he could see the saint. When he was received, he was so pleased that he pressed on Amardas a gift of several villages, but the Guru answered :

> 'I have obtained lands and rentfree holdings from my Creator
> 'He who cherisheth all existences giveth also unto me.
> 'Whatever cometh daily is spent daily and for the morrow my trust is in God.'

The emperor no longer pressed the Guru but made a gift of several villages to Amardas's daughter Bhani.

Amardas seems early to have made up his mind to appoint his son-in-law Jetha as his successor ; for he bade him leave Goindwal and build a great city on his wife's lands. When Jetha had built several houses, Amardas told him to excavate two tanks. One was to be named Santokshar or the Lake of Consolation, the other Amritsar or the Lake of Nectar. Thus was the famous city of Amritsar founded. Before finally appointing Jetha, Amardas resolved to test both him and his other son-in-law Rama. He bade them each build him a platform, in order that he might sit on one in the morning and on the other in the evening. Rama's platform was completed first; but the Guru objected to it and bade him pull it down and build another. Rama did so; but the Guru was again displeased and made him pull it down again. Rama obeyed; but when the Guru objected for the third time to the platform, Rama pulled it down, but would not rebuild it, saying, 'The Guru hath grown old and his reason faileth.'

The Guru then treated Jetha in the same way. No less than seven times did Jetha without a murmur pull down and rebuild his platform. At last the Guru embraced him and said, 'Obeying my order, seven times hast thou built the platform, so seven generations of thine shall sit on the Guru's throne.' Agreeably to this promise the Guru in September, A.D. 1574, formally declared Jetha to be his successor, but under his real name Ramdas. Two days later Amardas died.

TEACHERS OF THE PUNJAB

13. Guru Ramdas

By the time Ramdas had been named Guru, the Sikh religion had grown like a mighty tree from the tiny seed sown by Guru Nanak. An important question arose in the Sikh community as to the value of pilgrimages and whether Sikhs should, as other Hindus did, visit the holy places of India. Ramdas decided against pilgrimages, thereby dividing his flock more sharply from the orthodox Hindus. He said :

> 'They who go on a pilgrimage commit every kind of wickedness.
> 'The good acts they do are merely for show.
> 'They give alms to those who flatter them to their faces or to others.
> 'How shall persons such as these be saved?'

One day Sri Chand, the elder son of Guru Nanak, went to visit Guru Ramdas. Sri Chand had not acquiesced in his supersession by Angad and leaving his father's sect had founded one of his own, known as the Udasis or persons indifferent to this world. He taught his followers to wander naked, clothed only by the surrounding universe. Sri Chand had no quarrel with Ramdas and he decided to visit him. After the customary greetings Sri Chand said to his host, 'What a long beard you have grown !' 'Yes,' replied the modest Guru, 'I have grown a long beard that I may wipe thy feet!' and he actually did wipe Sri Chand's feet with his beard. This act of humility quite disarmed Sri Chand, who in turn admitted Ramdas's right to the headship of the Sikh community.

Ramdas always preached against the ascetic life and pressed his Sikhs to marry and beget children and not to waste their lives in idle asceticism. One day some yogis said that the Sikhs could not win salvation because they led worldly lives. Ramdas replied:

> 'As the teats on a goat's neck yield no milk, so Yog without piety yieldeth no advantage.
>
> 'My Sikhs have wives and children and yet will obtain salvation.
>
> 'It would be impossible for them to practise Yog.'

A charming story is told how Ramdas cured a leper. The Kardar or revenue officer of Pattia, a town in the Lahore district, had five daughters. Four of them were married, but the fifth and youngest was not even betrothed. One day all five went for a bath and a picnic to their father's country house. On the way home they heard some Sikh saints singing the hymns of Nanak. They produced no effect on the four married daughters; but they so inspired the virgin girl that she took off her cloak and jewels and gave them to the saints. On reaching home she began a series of edifying discourses to her sisters. Her mother was much annoyed that her daughter should turn preacher. She told her husband, who sent for all his daughters. He asked them who fed, clothed and protected them. The four married daughters bowed to the ground and said that their parents had done so. The youngest daughter answered, 'The One God alone is the Cherisher of Creation. Parents are only a pretext.' Her father was very angry and said, 'Who hath given thee clothes and jewels?' She replied, 'My father, all these are God's gifts. He giveth to thee and to me and protecteth us all.' The father was in a great rage and shouted at her, 'We shall see if God will protect thee.' Some days afterwards a leprous cripple came begging through the town. The vindictive father saw a chance of gratifying his spite. He compelled his daughter to marry the wretched man, stripped her of her clothes and without giving her any money turned her out of the house.

The unhappy girl did what she could for her husband and went begging with him. One day her husband, who, to do him justice, fully appreciated his bride's devotion, expressed a wish to go on a pilgrimage and so acquire merit. This would perhaps bring him in the next life the happiness that had been denied to him in this. But he was a cripple and so he could not walk. The brave-hearted girl got a basket big enough to hold him. He sat in it and she lifted him on her head. In this way she took him to Hardwar, Tribeni and other sacred places. At last she brought him to Amritsar, where Guru Ramdas was watching the completion of the Amrita Lake. She put him down in the shade of a *ber* tree and went to the nearest village to beg food. While the leper was awaiting her return, he saw two crows fighting for a morsel of bread. It dropped into the water of the half finished tank. Both birds plunged after it. When they came out again, they were no longer crows, but beautiful white swans. In this new guise they flew northwards, never resting until they had reached Manas Sarovar, the holy lake beyond the Himalayas. The leper thought that water of such singular efficacy might perhaps cure him of his horrible disease. Crawling to the bank, he seized with one hand a branch of the *ber* tree and let himself sink into the water. Not only did his leprosy at once leave him, but his crippled limbs became straight and beautiful. Only one part remained unhealed and that was the hand by which he had held the branch of the *ber* tree. When his wife returned, she could not believe that he was her husband and indignantly rejected both his story and his embraces. She charged him with having killed her leper in order to marry her. At last her husband induced her to go with him to consult Guru Ramdas, who was seated under a tree not far away. After greeting the Guru, the young wife told her version of what had happened and scouted as impossible the magic qualities of the pool. The Guru smiled and said, 'Nay, we can easily test the truth of your husband's tale. One of his hands is still covered with leprous sores. Let him dip it in the water and we shall see whether it gets well or not.' Both husband and wife accepted the test. The former dipped into the water his festering hand and it was immediately healed. The wife at once believed her husband's story and was overjoyed. She took him to her father, who adopted as his son, his now beautiful son-in-law. Making over to him all his property, the father became a devout follower of Guru Ramdas. The *ber* tree to which the crippled husband clung still stands; and the spot is known as Dukhbhanjani or destroyer of sorrow.

As Guru Ramdas grew old, the question of his succession arose. In view of Guru Amardas' prophecy the choice lay between his two sons Prithia and Arjan. The former was the elder but avaricious and self-seeking. Arjan the younger was in every way fitted to sit on the Guru's throne. This was proved not long before Guru Ramdas' death. One day Saharimal, the Guru's first cousin, came from Lahore to invite the Guru to his son's wedding. Ramdas could not himself leave Amritsar, so he asked Prithia to represent him at the marriage feast. But Prithia was misappropriating for himself so large a share of the Guru's offerings, that he had no wish to leave Amritsar. He also feared for the succession, in case Ramdas died in his absence. Prithia, therefore, made so many excuses, that the Guru sent his younger Arjan instead. Arjan went gladly and stayed on at Lahore some time after the wedding. At length he grew homesick and wrote thus to his father :

> 'My soul longeth for a sight of the Guru
> 'It crieth like a *chatak* bird for raindrops
> 'My thirst is not quenched, and I have no rest without a sight of my beloved saint.
> 'I am a sacrifice, I am a sacrifice to a sight of the Guru, the beloved and holy one.'

Prithia met the messenger. Unable to write verse himself, he was filled with jealousy at his brother's poetic talents. He took the letter and hid it, ordering the messenger to tell Arjan that his father wished him to stay at Lahore. The messenger went back and told Arjan what had happened. Arjan wrote a second letter in verse, which Prithia also intercepted. Arjan wrote a third letter marked No. 3 and told the messenger to give it to none save the Guru in person. Prithia waited for the messenger, but the latter hid and evaded him. Then the messenger made his way to the Guru and gave him the letter. He also told him how Prithia had intercepted the other two missives and pointed to the No. 3 as proof. When Prithia came, the Guru asked him for the other two letters. Prithia swore that he had lost them, but the Guru knew by his inner wisdom that they were in the pocket of Prithia's coat, then hanging from a peg in his bedroom. He sent a servant for Prithia's coat and found in one of the pockets the missing papers. After this exposure the Guru refused to name Prithia his successor. He sent for Arjan from Lahore. When Arjan came, his father said, 'Guru Amardas declared that the Guruship was the reward of merit. As only he who is lowly and humble-minded can claim it, I grant it to thee.' With these words he formally installed Arjan as his successor.

Prithia bore badly his supersession and spoke so offensively to and of his father that Guru Ramdas ordered him out of his sight, saying, 'Thou art a *Mina* (robber). My Sikhs will not obey thee ; they will never associate with thee.' After expelling Prithia, Ramdas left Amritsar and went to Goindwal and there feasted his closest followers. After the feast he addressed them and bade them accept Arjan as their Guru. To Arjan he gave the express command to complete the two tanks at Amritsar. In August 1581 Guru Ramdas passed away amid great sorrow ; for he was much beloved. The poet

Mathura composed the following lines on his death :

> 'Guru Ramdas who was pleasing to God went to God's city
> 'God gave him a throne and seated him on it.
> 'During thy life the sins of the demons trembled within them and they fled.
> 'The sins of those who received Guru Ramdas's instruction were cut away.
> 'He gave the umbrella and sovereignty of the earth to Guru Arjan.'

TEACHERS OF THE PUNJAB

14. Guru Arjan

The life of Guru Arjan was plagued by the ceaseless enmity of his brother Prithia. The latter never admitted Arjan's right to succeed their father. Immediately on Guru Ramdas' death Prithia complained to the *chaudhris* or village officers of Amritsar that he and Mahadev (his second brother) had been left entirely without means. The *chaudhris* spoke to Guru Arjan and he bestowed certain rents and taxes on Prithia and the customs duties of a single quarter of Amritsar on Mahadev. Arjan reserved for himself the voluntary offerings of the faithful. This gift for the time being calmed Prithia ; for he hoped that as Guru Arjan had no son, his own son Mihrban would obtain the succession.

Guru Arjan devoted all his energies to the completion of the Amritsar tank that Guru Ramdas had left unfinished, and to the construction of the holy Har Mandar, better known as the Darbar Sahib or the Golden Temple of Amritsar. He sent agents, who collected money from the hill-chiefs and a rich corn merchant called Ganga Ram gave him substantial help. When the tank had been completed, the great Har Mandar was begun. The Sikhs urged that to show its superiority over other buildings in Amritsar, the Har Mandar should overtop them all. The Guru replied with admirable humility :

> 'No ! What is humble shall be exalted. The more a tree is laden with fruit, the more its branches droop earthwards.

> 'From whatever point you come to the temple, you must go down eight steps; therefore let the Har Mandar be the lowest building of them all.'

In the design of the Har Mandar, Guru Arjan made an important departure from the ordinary temple. Hindu temples are closed on three sides and open only to the east or the rising sun. The great Sikh temple was built open on all sides. This signified that the Sikh faith was open to all and had nothing to do with sun-worship. On the first Magh, St. 1643 (February or January, A.D. 1589), Guru Arjan laid the first brick of the Golden Temple. A mason accidentally displaced the brick, whereupon Guru Arjan prophesied that the foundations would some time have to be relaid. This prophecy came true. In A.D. 1763 the Afghan king Ahmad Shah Abdali destroyed the temple and defiled the tank. Two years later when the Sikhs recovered the ruins, they relaid the foundations and rebuilt the temple. In the meantime, however, the work progressed so quickly that Guru Arjan felt sure that divine hands were helping him. In his gratitude he wrote a poem of which the following lines may be quoted :

> 'God Himself came, and stood up to do the work of the saints.
> 'Into the beautiful earth and the beautiful lake He poured nectarlike water.
> 'He poured water like nectar, finished the work and gratified our desires
> 'To bathe in this tank is the same as bathing in the sixty-eight places of pilgrimage, as the bestowal of alms and the performance of great purification.'

So long as no son was born to Arjan and his wife Ganga, Prithia did not actively quarrel with his brother. Prithia's wife Karmo was bitterly jealous of Ganga and did her utmost, by exaggerating Arjan's riches and the great value of his offerings, to foment the feud. But Prithia used to calm her by saying, 'Thou hast the greatest wealth of all in son Mihrban. When he grows up, he shall be Guru. Arjan has no son and his reign shall be short.'

After some years Ganga bore her lord a son named Har Gobind. The news of this event filled Prithia and Karmo with anger and Prithia's dislike of his brother turned to malignant hatred. He made various efforts to poison Har Gobind. Once he sent a nurse with poison smeared on her bosom to suckle his little nephew ; but before she could give the child her breast, she fell back in a faint. When she recovered, she confessed the wicked deed she had come to do. Another time Prithia offered a snake charmer a large reward to kill Har Gobind by snake bite. The snake-charmer let loose a cobra close to where the little boy sat. The cobra rushed towards Har Gobind, but he took it in his little hands and tore it to pieces. A third time Prithia hired a Brahman to poison the child's milk ; but the Guru who suspected the Brahman gave some to a dog and it died in agony. After these failures Prithia left the child alone and Guru Arjan began the sacred book known as the *Granth Sahib*.

Guru Nanak had invented a special script called Gurmukhi (*Guru Mukhi*=from the mouth of the Guru) for the Sikh hymns and psalms. In this script Guru Arjan gathered together the sayings and acts of the great teachers, who had preceded him ; but it was too holy a work to be written in an ordinary spot. He chose carefully a hermitage in the forest conspicuous for its sylvan beauty. To add to its charm he had a lake dug known as the Ramsar Lake. On its completion he began collecting materials for the *Granth Sahib*.

Everything so far had prospered with Guru Arjan, when an unlucky fate brought on him the bitter enmity of the emperor's Diwan, Chandu Shah. The latter was rich, well born and accomplished and Fortune seemed ever to smile on him. Unhappily he had a daughter aged seven called Sada Kaur. He was anxious to get her a husband, as Musulmans often carried off and converted to Islam unmarried Hindu girls. Chandu sent his family priest and his barber to look for a husband. These two worthies searched everywhere and found none so suitable as Har Gobind, the son of Guru Arjan. They went back and sang the praises of father and son so loudly that they roused Chandu's jealousy. He spoke scornfully of the Guru, alleging that his caste was too low. 'Thou wishest,' he said to the priest, 'to put the ornamental tile of a top storey into the gutter.' Chandu reluctantly consented. All would then have been well had Chandu's words not been repeated to the Sikhs. They were justly angry and pressed the Guru to break off the match. He allowed himself to be persuaded and told Chandu's priest that he had no wish to put an ornamental tile into the gutter. The answer was approved by the Sikhs present and one rose and said, 'Great King, put not acid into milk. Spurn an alliance with that dog of a Karar (*bania*).' Two other wives were offered to the Guru for Har Gobind by Sikhs present; and the match-makers, the priest and the barber, returned disconsolately to Delhi where they reported all that had happened.

Chandu Shah was very angry; but he tried to smooth matters over by writing to Guru Arjan and withdrawing all that he had said. He also threatened that he would in the absence of a settlement, become Prithia's ally. The letter received no written reply. Chandu Shah now became the deadly enemy of Guru Arjan. He got the emperor Akbar to summon Arjan to court on a charge of heresy; but when his writings and those of the other Gurus were examined, the tolerant Akbar found no fault with them. He dismissed the Guru with many and costly presents.

Shortly afterwards the great Akbar died and his son Jahangir reigned in his stead. Jahangir's son Khusru rebelled. Beaten in the field, Khusru fled towards Afghanistan. On the way he passed the Guru's dwelling place and pleading great poverty induced the Guru to give him five thousand rupees. The gift proved useless to Prince Khusru, for he was afterwards taken alive; and the Guru's enemies used the gift as a weapon against the generous giver. Prithia died about this time, but his son Mihrban kept the feud alive. He told Chandu Shah of the aid given to the prince and Chandu told Jahangir. The emperor sent for the Guru and rebuked him for helping the rebel. The Guru met the imperial wrath with undaunted courage. He replied:

> 'If I had not assisted him (Khusru) in his forlorn condition and so shown some regard for the kindness of thy father the Emperor Akbar to myself, all men would have despised me for my heartlessness and ingratitude; or they would have said that I was afraid of thee. This would have been unworthy of a follower of Guru Nanak'

The emperor was not appeased by these brave words. He ordered Guru Arjan to pay a fine of two lakhs of rupees and to erase from the *Granth Sahib* all hymns opposed to the Hindu and Musulman religions. The heroic Guru refused to do either. Nor would he allow his Sikhs to subscribe the fine among themselves. He was then handed over to the keeping of Chandu Shah. The latter having got into his power his hated enemy, began at once to torture him. His agents poured burning sand on their victim, seated him on redhot cauldrons and plunged him in boiling water. The Guru never gratified his tormentors with either a sigh or a groan. Chandu Shah offered to stop the torture, if the Guru would consent to Har Gobind's marriage to Sada Kaur ; but this offer the Guru also rejected. Further cruel tortures followed. At last the Guru asked for and got leave to bathe in the River Ravi. Slowly with painful steps the suffering saint dragged himself to the edge of the river. He bathed in the cold water, but the hand of death was on him. This he knew and he told it to the Sikhs near him and he bade them appoint Har Gobind as his successor.

> 'Bid him not mourn,' he said, 'or indulge in unmanly lamentations, but sing God's praises. . . .
>
> 'Let him sit fully armed on his throne and maintain the strongest army that he can.'

So Sikhism passed from a sect of devotees to a a military organization. On the 4th of the first half of Jeth (June 1606) Guru Arjan passed away. During his life he finished the Amritsar Tank, he built the Golden Temple and began the *Granth Sahib*. By his death he gave to his disciples an immortal example of loyalty, faith and courage.

TEACHERS OF THE PUNJAB

15. Guru Har Gobind

The new spiritual leader of the Sikhs was suited both in body and temper to carry out his father's wishes and maintain an army. Instead of wearing the cord and turban of his predecessors, he, after his father's funeral rites were over, sent for arms and armour and donning them, appeared in so martial a guise, that the Sikh chronicler speaks of him as shining like the sun. Nor was he content with wearing armour, he soon enrolled several hundred men, giving to each a horse and a weapon. When asked how he would feed them, he quoted the lines of Guru Arjan :

> 'God putteth their food even before the insects which He created in rocks and stones.
>
> 'He provideth everyone with his daily food; why, O Man, art thou afraid?'

Chandu became alarmed at the growing power of his dead enemy's son and made a last effort to conciliate him and induce him to marry his still unwedded daughter. He could not resist adding a threat that unless Har Gobind consented, he would treat Har Gobind as he had treated Guru Arjan. The spirited young Sikh wrote a haughty reply in which he not only rejected Chandu's offer, but threatened a fearful vengeance for the tortures inflicted on his father. 'Thou shalt die,' he wrote, 'trodden in the dust and dishonoured by shoe beatings inflicted by pariahs.'

Chandu became, on receiving this reply, as bitter an enemy of Guru Har Gobind as he had been of his unhappy father. He told the Emperor Jahangir of the troops raised by Har Gobind and, of course, enormously exaggerated their numbers. He warned the emperor that unless he took instant measures the whole Punjab would be in flames. The emperor alarmed at the news, summoned Guru Har Gobind to court. High debate took place at Amritsar when the emperor's summons came. Many Sikhs urged Har Gobind to disobey it; but that would have meant open insurrection. Har Gobind wisely obeyed the order and after leaving strict orders as to the management in his absence of the Har Mandar, he set out for Delhi. A lucky accident enabled the Guru to save the emperor's life when hunting. The emperor had heard that Har Gobind loved the chase and took him out to beat for tigers. A wounded tiger charged the emperor and was at the last moment killed by a sword cut of the Guru. This brave act probably saved the Guru from his father's fate; even as it was, he was imprisoned in the Gwalior fort through the machinations of Chandu.

In Gwalior the Guru found a number of unfortunate rajas and nobles imprisoned. Their only crime had been to own territories that the imperial government coveted. The Guru won the prisoners' esteem by supplying them with good food and clean clothes. Fortunately, too, the governor of the fort Haridas had long been a Sikh in secret and rejoiced greatly at the coming of the Guru. He went out to meet his prisoner, prostrated himself before him and sprinkled the dust from the Guru's feet over his own head and body. Chandu thought that once Har Gobind was inside the Gwalior fort his murder would be easy. He offered Haridas an income of five thousand rupees a year, if the latter would murder his prisoner. Haridas showed the letter to the Guru. Shortly afterwards Chandu sent a poisoned robe for the Guru to wear, but Haridas told this also to the Guru. At last the Guru's friends at court, of whom Wazir Khan, a powerful noble, was one obtained his release. The Guru went to Delhi to thank the emperor. The latter noted a beautiful rosary of yellow wooden beads that the Guru wore and asked for it as a keepsake. The Guru replied that his father had worn a far more beautiful rosary all of pearls and that he wished to give that to the emperor. The latter asked where it was. The Guru replied that Chandu had it, having stolen it from Guru Arjan's neck. The emperor asked Chandu to bring it. The latter went to his house but came back without it, pretending that he had lost it. In his absence Guru Har Gobind told Jahangir all the sufferings of his father. The capricious emperor at once changed his views and from being friendly to Chandu became very bitter against him. When Chandu came back without the necklace, the emperor bade Har Gobind take him away and take vengeance on him for his father's terrible end. Har Gobind at first refused, quoting the lines of Guru Ramdas :

'The true Guru is generous and compassionate; he feeleth compassion ever.

'The true Guru wisheth well to all; how could any evil befall him?'

At last Har Gobind consented to take Chandu away with him to Amritsar; but no sooner had the Sikhs seized Chandu than they made him expiate his cruelty to Guru Arjan. They pelted him with mud and filth. They had him beaten by pariahs with slippers. Then they took him round daily to beg food. At last death came to release him. A grain parcher, enraged at the sight of the wicked man, fractured his skull with an iron ladle. Sweepers threw his body into the River Ravi.

Although Chandu had thus suffered for his sins, the Guru had still two enemies alive. One was Prithia's son Mihrban and the other Chandu's son Karamchand. Guru Har Gobind tried to win over Mihrban by quoting to him a couplet of Kabir:

> 'Indulge not in envy and bribery, O my Soul,
> 'Do good deeds and gain their reward.'

Prithia's hatred was too intense to be cured by couplets and he drove away his cousin the Guru with contumely. Not long afterwards Jahangir died in Kashmir and his son Shah Jahan succeeded to the vacant throne. Mihrban and Karamchand lost no time in poisoning the new emperor's mind against the Guru. One day Shah Jahan had gone hunting from Lahore towards Amritsar. The Guru, unaware of the emperor's movements, chanced to go hunting from Amritsar towards Lahore. Now it so happened that the Shah of Persia had given to Shah Jahan a beautiful white hunting hawk. Towards the end of the hunt a Brahmani duck rose from a pool close by. The emperor ordered the white hawk to be set at the duck; but the hawk had been spoilt by its keeper and instead of striking down the duck played with it. The emperor grew impatient and rode back to Lahore, leaving some men to look for the hawk. The duck flew away with the hawk after it, until both birds came to where the Guru rode. He, seeing the duck, let loose one of his own hawks and it instantly struck down the quarry. The white hawk flew to earth after the duck and the Sikhs caught it as well as the Guru's hawk. A little later the emperor's men rode up and claimed the white hawk. The Sikhs retorted that the white hawk was, when they caught it, a wild bird and that the emperor had lost all ownership in it. The imperial hawk keepers would not admit this plea and hot words ensued. Blows followed words. The Sikhs beat off the imperial servants, killing several of their number. The survivors rode back to Lahore, where they reported the loss of the hawk and the deaths of their companions. The emperor, already suspicious of the Guru, sent against him one Mukhlis Khan with seven thousand men. It is not my task to describe in detail the fighting between the Sikhs and the emperor's troops. The latter were too few to overthrow the powerful force that the Guru had organized. Mukhlis Khan was killed by the Guru himself and his army beaten (A.D. 1628). No less than three times afterwards the Guru won pitched battles against the imperial troops. Had the emperor been wise, he would have concentrated the whole power of the empire and destroyed the Sikhs before they became a real danger. He had too many other matters on his hands to do so and the Guru, until his death, remained unbeaten.

The Guru had three wives, Damodari by whom

he had a son Gurditta, Nanaki by whom he had three sons Ani Rai, Teg Bahadur and Atal Rai, and Marwahi by whom he had a son Surajmal. Gurditta came by an untimely end when only twenty-four. He had been hunting and during the chase one of his Sikhs killed a cow in mistake for a deer. The cowherds seized the unskilful shot and would not free him, unless Gurditta restored the cow to life. This Gurditta, although he had the power, did not wish to do as the Guru his father disliked such miracles. At last to save his follower, he put his cane on the cow's head and said, 'Arise and eat grass.' At these words the cow got up and joined the herd. The Guru was very angry when he heard of the miracle. He said, 'It is not pleasing to me that you should set yourself up as God's equal and restore life to the dead.' Gurditta was deeply affected at his father's rebuke. He took his leave respectfully and walked to the shrine of Budhan Shah. There driving his cane into the ground, he lay down and died of a broken heart.

On Gurditta's death, his eldest son Dhirmal should ordinarily have been Har Gobind's successor. He stole the *Granth Sahib*, thinking thereby to make certain of the succession. His ambition defeated itself and Har Gobind chose his younger grandson Har Rai to succeed him. When Har Gobind was dying, Har Rai asked him what he should do if the emperor attack him. Har Gobind replied, 'God will be with thee and assist thee. Keep ever by thy side two thousand two hundred mounted soldiers.'

Guru Har Gobind died in A.D. 1645 after a spiritual and temporal reign of thirty-seven years and ten months. He was a great man, a fine soldier and a skilful captain. A Sikh poet Bhai Gur Das has briefly summed up the qualities of the first six Gurus and it would be hard to better his lines.

> 'The divine Nanak Guru was the Guru of Gurus.
> 'In an unseen and inscrutable manner he was absorbed in Angad,
> 'Who was absorbed in an unseen and invisible manner in Amar the Immortal,
> 'The nectar trickled into the mouth of him who was called Ramdas, the destroyer of enemies.
> 'Guru Arjan by serving him bore his burden,
> 'Guru Har Gobind the measureless churned the nectar and took his seat on Eternal Truth.'

TEACHERS OF THE PUNJAB

16. GURU HAR RAI

GURU Har Rai was born in Magh or February, A.D. 1631, of Gurditta's wife Nihal Kaur or Natti. He was more inclined to devotion than his grandfather Har Gobind and less to hunting and martial exercises. Still he retained the bodyguard of two thousand two hundred horsemen and he went hunting; but the beasts that he caught he did not slay. He took them back with him and kept them in his zoological gardens. In the evening he would hold his court and listen to hymns and impart instruction. A favourite couplet of his was from the poems of Guru Arjan :

> 'Learn the word, my Beloved, which is our support in life and death.
> 'By remembering the One God your faces shall ever be bright and happy.'

It was not long before his powers as a healer were tested. Prince Aurangzib, to get rid of Prince Dara Shukoh, his father's favourite son, had put, so the story runs, some tiger's whiskers in his brother's food. Dara Shukoh got very ill and the wisest doctors in the land decided that only one medicine would cure him. It was a myrabolam weighing twenty-eight ounces and a clove weighing one masha. Such an enormous myrabolam and so vast a clove were nowhere to be found. The emperor was advised to apply to Guru Har Rai. This Shah Jahan was at first reluctant to do; but at last he pocketed his pride and sent the Guru a humble letter. The Guru showed his forgiveness by quoting the line:

'Why should they, who come with hope, depart disappointed?' He produced from his store-house a myrabolam and a clove of the size needed. To these he added a pearl to be ground into powder and mixed with the other medicines. The imperial messenger took the drugs back to Delhi; they drove the tiger's whiskers out of the Prince's system and he regained his health.

One day the Guru when out hunting met a wounded snake. It was crawling with difficulty and was suffering tortures from maggots. The Guru granted the snake not only freedom from pain but salvation; and his astonished Sikhs saw its spirit soar, a bright light, into the heavens. They asked the Guru what the light was. He explained that in the time of Nanak Guru the wounded snake had been a Pandit and had bragged about the Vedas and his own powers. He went so far as to maintain that he was God on earth. He would sneer at Guru Nanak's hymns because they were written in the vulgar tongue, ignorant that they far surpassed the Vedas. As a punishment the Pandit had become a snake and the maggots in his wounds were the penalty of his sins. As, however, in a still earlier life, he had done some good deeds, he had been permitted to meet Guru Har Rai and win salvation. The Guru then quoted the lines of Guru Arjan.

> 'Though one be very beautiful, of high birth, clever, rich and of divine speech,
> 'Yet shall he be deemed as dead, O Nanak, if he have no love for God.'

The time came when the splendid Shah Jahan fell ill and his sons struggled for the throne. To use the words of the Sikh chronicler 'In every village men's minds were as unsettled as a boat in a whirlpool.' Aurangzib's forces won and Dara Shukoh became a fugitive. All villages and towns were closed against him. In his despair he remembered the Guru, who had cured him of the illness caused by the tiger's whiskers. He begged help from Guru Har Rai. The Guru could not promise him earthly glory, but he wrote :

> 'O Prince, thou art the object of God's grace. In the desire to tread in God's way and to know thyself, thou hast obtained spiritual empire.
>
> 'Aurangzib, who is unmindful of God, may obtain worldly empire, but shall suffer without respite in Hell fire.'

Dara Shukoh and the Guru met on the right bank of the Bias River. The Guru welcomed warmly the enlightened and tolerant prince and bade him be of good cheer and fight on ; but Aurangzib was in hot pursuit and before Dara Shukoh could raise fresh armies, he was hunted from place to place and finally taken through treachery. He was dragged to Delhi and executed. The storm of the imperial anger next burst on Guru Har Rai. He was summoned to Delhi. The Guru refused to go. Aurangzib then sent him a soothing letter, hoping to entrap him. The Guru was too wise to trust the bigoted emperor. He sent his eldest son Ram Rai instead. The emperor received Ram Rai courteously, but tried secretly to murder him. He sent Ram Rai poisoned robes, but the youth wore them without any ill effects. Aurangzib then had a deep pit dug in front of his throne and covered it with a sheet. He bade Ram Rai come near him. Ram Rai walked over the sheet, but it bore him safely. At last the emperor resolved to ensnare Ram Rai into speaking heresy. He quoted to Ram Rai a couplet from Guru Nanak :

> 'The ashes of the Musulman fall into the potter's clod,
> Vessels and bricks are fashioned from them; they cry out as they burn.'

'What does this mean?' asked the emperor. Ram Rai with ready wit said that the word 'Musulman' was an error. In the original the word was 'Beiman' or unfaithful. This satisfied the emperor; but in satisfying the emperor, Ram Rai committed a grave sin. Before Ram Rai had set out for Delhi, his father had warned him not to change by one jot or tittle the words of the Gurus. The young man's lapse was reported to Guru Har Rai, who was greatly affected by it. He resolved to exclude Ram Rai and give the succession to Har Krishan his second son. 'The Guruship,' said the Guru, 'is like tiger's milk, that can only be contained in a golden cup. Only he who is ready to devote his life to it is worthy of it. Let Ram Rai not look on my face again. Let him abide with Aurangzib and amass money at his court. In the words of Guru Amardas :

> 'Let him who is worthy sit on the king's throne
> 'The face of the liar shall be cursed; the true saint only shall be magnified.'

Ram Rai did not give up the succession without a struggle. He asked for and obtained the intercession of his uncle Dhir Mal and of his grandmother

Natti. Many Sikhs, too, because of the favour shown to Ram Rai by the terrible emperor, thought it good policy that Ram Rai should succeed. It was to no purpose. When Guru Har Rai felt his end near, he resolved to appoint Har Krishan his successor without delay. He summoned a great council of Sikhs thinking of the words of Kabir :

> 'Do now the work of to-morrow; and if thou do it now, do it at once.
> 'Nothing can be done hereafter, when death standeth by thy head.'

In the presence of the assembled magnates, Har Rai seated Har Krishan, still a child, on the throne. He put a coco-nut and five paise before him and walked round him three times. Lastly he had a *tilak* put on Har Krishan's forehead. The whole company rose and did the young Guru obeisance. Guru Har Rai did not long survive the ceremony. In Kartik or November, A.D. 1661, Guru Har Rai passed away.

TEACHERS OF THE PUNJAB

17. Guru Har Krishan

The life story of Guru Har Krishan is a tragedy. He was only a child of five when he became Guru and death removed him when a child of nine. He was the second son of Guru Har Rai and his wife Krishan Kaur. As already related, he was appointed to the succession by his father because of the errors of Ram Rai. Ram Rai, however, did not acquiesce in his supersession. He proclaimed himself Guru and fell into the hands of greedy disciples. They went through the land extorting large sums of money. Of the money so extorted they only gave a fraction to Ram Rai. The rest they kept themselves.

Ram Rai resolved to lay his case before Aurangzib. The latter saw in the quarrels of the brothers, if artfully fomented, a means of destroying the Sikh power. He summoned Har Krishan to his court. The child Guru was wise beyond his years. He agreed to go to Delhi, provided he was invited by the Sikhs of Delhi and not by the emperor. An invitation was accordingly sent to the Guru through the Raja Jai Singh of Jaipur, as if from the Delhi Sikhs; and the little Guru accepted it. When Guru Har Krishan had reached a spot called Panjokhare, a proud Brahman heard of him and got very angry that his name was Sri Har Krishan. 'The author of the *Bhagwat Gita,*' said the Brahman, 'was just Krishna, but this boy would call himself also Sri, which means Laxmi and Har which means Shiva. He therefore, deems himself greater than Krishna.' The Brahman resolved to teach the Guru a lesson and forced his way into his presence. There he did not salute the Guru, but sat down rudely in front of him. Then he said, 'Since thou callest thyself Sri Har Krishna, thou must think thyself greater than Kṛishna. Come and read the *Bhagwat Gita* with me.' The Guru replied, 'I have not read the Gita; and were I to translate it with thee, thou wouldest say that I was some rich man's son, who had had a private tutor; whereas I translate by my spiritual power. Go and fetch some ignorant rustic with whom to discuss the Gita.' The Brahman fetched from the village a stupid water-carrier called Chajju. But the Guru inspired Chajju with his own supernatural powers and he gave such learned replies to the Brahman that the latter was beaten in argument and completely confounded. In the end he became the Guru's disciple.

When Har Krishan reached Delhi, the emperor asked him to court; but the little Guru firmly refused to go, urging that Ram Rai was at court and was more fitted to discuss high politics than himself. His own mission was to preach the True Name. At the request of one of the emperor's sons, he sent some lines from one of Guru Nanak's hymns to Aurangzib:

'If the True God dwell not in the heart
'What is eating, what is clothing?
'What is a pleasant couch for billing and cooing?
'What is an army, what are macebearers and servants and what are palaces to live in?'
'Nanak, except the True Name all things are perishable.'

The emperor was much impressed by the poem and by the intelligence of the child, who had quoted it. He wished further to test the spiritual powers of the little Guru. In consultation with Raja Jai Singh the emperor made a trial of him. When the little Guru visited Jai Singh's palace, he was to be led into the presence of the Raja's queens and their attendants. The head queen was to dress herself as a servant and sit at the back. The Raja would see whether Har Krishan could penetrate the disguise or not. The little Guru saw through the childish plot and detected at once the chief Rani in spite of her menial clothing. By passing the test, he convinced the Raja and his queens of his sainthood.

The rich promise of the Guru's childhood was never to be fulfilled. On the day after his visit to the Raja's zanana he developed fever. Next morning small-pox showed itself. The little patient bore his illness with the courage of his forerunners. He uttered neither moans nor cries, but continually repeated the name of the Most High. In spite of his sickness he had to name a successor. The suffering child called for five paise and a coco-nut. He waved with difficulty his hand three times in the air and said, 'Baba Bakali,' meaning thereby to appoint his great uncle Teg Bahadur who lived in Bakala village. Feeling that he could never again be well, he quoted a couplet from Guru Arjan :

> 'Where the physician cannot succeed, where there is neither sister nor brother, God alone assisteth,
> 'What He doeth cometh to pass, He washeth away the stains of sin. Forget not the Supreme Being.'

The Guru's last words were a command that none should weep for him. They were to sing hymns during his last agony; and in the midst of sacred music the child-saint passed away. It was on the 14th Chet, April, A.D. 1664.

GURU TEG BAHADUR

TEACHERS OF THE PUNJAB

18. Guru Teg Bahadur

Guru Teg Bahadur, the youngest son of the sixth Guru Har Gobind and his wife Nanaki, was born at Amritsar in Vaishakh or May, A.D. 1622. He was a fine strong boy for his age and his father Har Gobind prophesied that he would grow up a mighty hero. He gave him the name of Teg Bahadur or the Brave Sword and foretold that Teg Bahadur would beget a son, who would overthrow the Moghul tyranny.

When Guru Har Krishan died and his dying words 'Baba Bakala' were known, no less than twenty-two Sikhs of Bakala wrongfully declared themselves the occupants of the spiritual throne. Teg Bahadur, disgusted with their behaviour, shut himself in his house. The false gurus were at last confounded by one Makhan Shah. In imminent danger of shipwreck, he had vowed, if he escaped, to give five hundred gold mohurs to the Guru. He did escape and once safe on dry land he tried to find the Guru to whom he would pay the five hundred gold mohurs. Instead of one Guru, he found twenty-two. He tested them all in turn. He offered each of them two gold mohurs. These they greedily accepted, ignorant of his vow to give five-hundred. Makhan Shah felt sure that all the twenty-two were impostors. He asked whether there was no else in Bakala fit to be guru. He was told that there was one Teg Bahadur, a man in every way fitted to be guru; but he made no claim to be one. Makhan

Shah with difficulty obtained an interview with Teg Bahadur and offered him also two gold mohurs; but Teg Bahadur by his inner wisdom, knew that Makhan Shah had vowed five hundred. He at once said, 'Where are the five hundred gold mohurs thou didst promise when thy vessel was sinking?' Makhan Shah gladly paid him the promised money and ran as fast as he could on to the roof. There he waved a flag and shouted, 'I have found the Guru! I have found the Guru!' His choice was approved by all and, as the chronicler puts it, 'The twenty-two false gurus hid themselves as darkness vanishes before sun's rays.'

Dhir Mal was jealous of Teg Bahadur's succession and one of his followers went with twelve servants to kill the new Guru. The assassin fired and wounded Teg Bahadur, but not mortally. Makhan Shah and other Sikhs seized both Dhir Mal and his followers and would have hanged them; but Teg Bahadur ordered them to be released, saying nobly:

> 'To exercise forgiveness is a great act. To exercise forgiveness is to give alms. Forgiveness is equal to ablutions at all places of pilgrimages. Forgiveness ensureth Man's salvation. There is no virtue equal to forgiveness. Therefore generously practise it.'

Teg Bahadur went from Bakala to Amritsar, but the priests would not accept him and closed against him the doors of the temple. He therefore returned to Bakala, but this, too, he left because of the jealousy and hatred of the false gurus whom he had unmasked. He went from Bakala to Kiratpur and thence to a place six miles distant, where he founded the city of Anandpur (A.D. 1665).

One day as he was riding through a forest two

thieves, a Hindu and a Musulman, followed him, so as to steal his horse. At night the Guru lay down by his horse and went to sleep. Suddenly a tiger came out of a neighbouring thicket and prostrated itself three times before the sleeping Guru. This was too much for the Musulman, who promptly ran away. The Hindu, however, was stubborn in his evil doing and after the tiger had gone, he stole the Guru's horse. When the Guru awoke, his servants missed it. The Guru told them to search for it a few hundred yards to the north of his camp. They did so and found the thief and the horse motionless under a tree. They brought the thief to the Guru, who asked him why he had not galloped off. The thief explained that after he had ridden for a few minutes, he had become blind and had lost his way. At last in despair, he had stopped where the Guru's men found him. After telling the Guru this, the thief climbed a tree, broke off the top branch and, in an agony of remorse, impaled himself.

Thereafter Teg Bahadur visited Agra, Prayag, Gaya and Patna. At Patna Raja Ram Singh of Ambar visited him and asked for his help in conquering Kamrup, a province between India and Burma. The task was a hard one, for the king of Kamrup had just defeated an army led by Mir Jamla, one of Aurangzib's most skilful generals. The Guru replied, 'God's name is a cure for all diseases. Guru Nanak will assist thee and thou shalt conquer Kamrup.' He also agreed to go with Raja Ram Singh on the expedition.

When the imperial army reached the borders of Kamrup, the king, who was a great magician, used the most terrible spells and incantations to destroy it. His court wizards did likewise. They had proved successful against Mir Jamla; but owing to the presence of Guru Teg Bahadur they were powerless against Raja Ram Singh. To use the words of the chronicler, 'As ignorance pales before knowledge, so did the sorcerers fail and grow weary of their efforts.' In the end the king of Kamrup accepted the terms that Raja Ram Singh imposed on him by the counsel of the Guru. To celebrate the victory, the Guru asked that each soldier of the imperial forces should bring five shields full of earth to raise a monument to Nanak Guru. On the mound so erected Teg Bahadur built a pavilion that stands to this day. When the army was about to return, the news came to Teg Bahadur that his wife Gujari had given birth to a son, afterwards the renowned Har Gobind Singh.

Nothing in Teg Bahadur's life became him like the leaving of it. Towards its close the emperor Aurangzib gave orders for the conversion of the Hindus of Kashmir. These orders were so strictly carried out by his officer Sher Afghan Khan, that he had soon collected a hundred weight of *janves* or sacred strings taken from the necks of Hindu converts to Islam. The Kashmiris sent a deputation to Guru Teg Bahadur. He heard them sadly and was pondering on what course he should follow, when his little son Gobind Rai asked him why he looked so stern. The Guru petted his son and said, 'The world is grieved by persecution. He who is willing to sacrifice his life shall free the earth from the burden of her tormentors.' The child said, 'My father, who is more fitted than thou to do this, generous and brave as thou art?' The Guru realized that from the mouths of babes often comes wisdom. He told the Kashmiris to tell the emperor that they would embrace Islam if Teg Bahadur embraced it first. The emperor at once sent for Teg Bahadur.

Teg Bahadur obeyed the summons and had reached Agra when he was seized by the *kotwal* and taken to Delhi. There Teg Bahadur firmly refused to be converted. He was closely imprisoned. One day he made his way to the top storey of his prison and was seen to look towards the south, where stood the imperial *zanana*. This was reported to the emperor, who sent for the Guru and charged him with a grave breach of taste and propriety. To this Teg Bahadur gave the immortal answer that years later was to be the battle cry of Nicholson's Sikhs.

'O Emperor, I was on the top storey of my prison, but I was not looking at thy private rooms or the chambers of thy queens. I was looking towards the men of Europe, who are coming from beyond the seas; for they will tear down thy curtains and destroy thine empire.'

About the same time three of the Sikhs imprisoned with Teg Bahadur escaped. His jailors locked the Guru in an iron cage and tortured him cruelly. When he was on the point of death, he wrote to his son Gobind Rai the following couplet :

'My strength is done, I am in chains and I have no way out.
'Saith Nanak "God is my refuge." '

To this Gobind Rai wrote the first couplet that ever came from his pen.

'Strength is thine; thy fetters are loosed; thou hast every resource;
'Nanak, everything is in thy power; it is only thou who canst assist thyself.'

Teg Bahadur was pleased at his son's precocious wisdom and sent him five paise and a coconut as a sign of his appointment to the Guruship.

Since neither tortures nor imprisonment affected the resolution of the Guru, the emperor threatened to put him to death, unless he either renounced his faith or proved his saintship by working a miracle. The Guru refused to do either. 'I will never abandon my faith,' he said, 'I want no honour in this life; I want honour hereafter.' The emperor at once ordered his execution. The Guru was taken from his cage and publicly beheaded. The head fell under the executioner's stroke into the lap of a faithful disciple. A storm of dust arose and under cover of it, the Sikh ran with the head as fast as he could to Anandpur. Shortly afterwards five Sikhs took the saint's body in a cart and secretly burnt it inside their houses. The houses caught fire and hid their act. They collected the Guru's charred bones, put them in a copper pot and buried them. The spot is now covered by the shrine of Rakab Ganj.

Teg Bahadur's head was cremated at Anandpur. As it burnt, the Sikhs sang the hymns composed by the dead man and praised his kindly, noble nature. In due course Gobind Rai was proclaimed the tenth and as it turned out the last Guru. He summed up his dead father's merits in the following fine lines:

> 'Having broken his potsherd on the head of the king of Delhi, he departed to Paradise.
>
> 'No one else who has come into this world has acted like Teg Bahadur.
>
> 'There was weeping for him in the whole world, but there was rejoicing in Paradise.'

TEACHERS OF THE PUNJAB

19. GURU GOBIND SINGH

THE new Guru was admirably suited by nature to the times in which he lived. The Sikhs had become so numerous as to be a real danger to the Moghùl Government and if they were not to be destroyed for political reasons, they needed a military leader. In Gobind Rai they found such a leader. From his earliest years he practised archery and sword-play and he gathered round him a bodyguard of gallant youths, of whom the foremost were his cousins, the five sons of his aunt Viro. At the same time Gobind Rai was a prolific hymn writer and his songs were sung by the women of Lahore from their housetops.

In 1677 the young Guru took to wife a girl called Jito, the daughter of one Bhikkia of Lahore and not long afterwards a beautiful young woman called Sundari, the daughter of a newly made convert. Shortly after the new Guru's accession, Ratan Rai, the son of the Raja of Assam, came to see him. He brought numerous gifts, of which 'a small but sagacious elephant' was certainly the most remarkable. The animal wiped the Guru's shoes and then put them before him—the right and left shoes in their proper places. When the Guru shot an arrow, the elephant would retrieve it. It would pour water over the Guru's feet and wipe them with a towel. During a Durbar, it would wave a horsetail over the Guru's head and at night it would show the Guru the way to his room, holding in its trunk a lighted torch.

The Rajas in the neighbouring hills had long been jealous of the spread of the Sikh power. Their jealousy grew rapidly when they heard that Gobind Rai had procured a drum called Ranjit or the Victorious in battle. The beating of a drum is one way of declaring one's independence and one of the Hill Chiefs, Raja Bhim Chand of Kalchur, retaliated by demanding the surrender of the Guru's sagacious elephant as the price of peace. Nothing would induce the Guru to part with it and Bhim Chand and the other hill chiefs declared war. They were completely defeated by the Guru.

After this victory and a second one over a body of Musulmans, who came to extort tribute, the Guru wrote some hymns in which he denounced the worship of Hindu images :

> 'Some, worshipping stones put them on their heads, some hang *lingams* from their necks ;
>
> 'Some see God in the south, some bow their heads to the west.
>
> 'Some fools worship idols, others busy themselves with worshipping the dead.
>
> 'The whole world, entangled as it is in false ceremonies, hath not found God's secret.'

The Guru had always a great dislike for cutting the hair and he relied on ancient Hindu texts as well as the particular instances of Christ and Mahomed. At length he resolved to lay down that the unshaven head was one of the essentials of the Sikh religion. He invited a number of Sikhs at the time of the Vaisakh (May) fair to be present at Anandpur, unshaven and unshorn. On the morning after their arrival he held an open air gathering. Drawing his sword, he asked whether any Sikh was ready to die for him. First Daya Ram, a Sikh of Lahore, rose. The Guru took him inside a separate enclosure and pretended to kill him. Then the Guru went back and repeated the question. Dharma Das of Delhi rose in his place and was taken to the enclosure ; and the same pantomime continued until five Sikhs had seemingly been slaughtered. The startled crowd thought that the Guru had gone mad ; but the Guru went out again and led back the five Sikhs. He said : 'These shall lay anew the foundation of Sikhism and the true religion shall spread and become famous through the world.' He added that from Guru Nanak's time the Sikhs had drunk the water in which the Guru had washed his feet. That must be stopped ; humility must give place to valour. In future the Sikh nation must be baptized with water, stirred with a dagger. He abolished caste and discouraged pilgrimages. He then stirred some water in an iron vessel with his sword. His wife Jito threw some sweets into it and the Guru baptised the five disciples, calling them his Panch Pyare or five beloved and giving them the name of Singh or lion. He bade them always wear five things, all of which began with a 'K'--kes, or hair, kangha or comb, krifan or sword, kachh or short drawers, kara or a steel bracelet. The disciples in their turn baptized the Guru and from that time he too was known as Gobind Singh and no longer as Gobind Rai. To the body of Sikhs he gave the name of Khalsa. One Bhai Santokh Singh recorded this momentous event in the following couplets :

> 'God's Khalsa which has arisen is very holy. When its followers meet, they say "Wahguruji ki Fateh !"

'The Khalsa has done away with all regard for Pirs, spiritual rulers and miracle workers of other sects, whether Hindu or Musulman.

'The world on seeing a third religion was astonished; the foe feared that it would take away their dominion.'

All Sikhs were now ordered to give up caste and to receive the *pahul* or baptism of the dagger. Although caste prejudices stood for some time in the way, the great majority of the Punjab Sikhs received it. Those of Sind have not as a rule done so.

The new military organization of the Sikhs caused the greatest fear among the Hill Rajas. They called in the aid of the Moghuls. A large imperial force co-operated with them and besieged Anandpur. The pressure of the siege and hunger led many of the garrison to desert. At last the Guru, who had obstinately defended the fort prepared to leave it. His retreat was discovered. His army was destroyed. His sons Ajit Singh and Zoravar Singh were cut down. He himself was taken alive in the Patiala State by a detachment of imperial cavalry. He made good his escape by pretending to be a Musulman saint Uch ka Pir. In the meantime the Guru's mother Gujari and his two younger sons Jujhar Singh and Fateh Singh had entrusted themselves to a Brahman, who promised them shelter. He proved a faithless traitor. First he stole Gujari's money and when she charged him with the theft, he feigned great indignation and ordered her and the children to leave his house. Having turned them out penniless, he informed the governor of Murinda. The latter had them arrested and taken to Wazir Khan, the viceroy of Sarhind.

The cruel viceroy told the captives that Gobind

Singh, Ajit Singh and Zoravar Singh were all dead and that the children's only hope of life was in their acceptance of Islam. The elder child Jujhar Singh aged nine retorted proudly, 'My father, the holy Guru Gobind Singh is not dead. Who can kill him? He is protected by the Immortal God.' The bravery of the little boy filled the spectators with pity; but a wretch named Sachanand Khatri, who had in vain asked for one of the Guru's sons for his daughter pressed for the children's instant execution. 'They are the offspring of a serpent,' said Sachanand, 'when they grow up they will be serpents even as their father is.' The viceroy offered the children death or Islam. Jujhar Singh answered in words that still stir the heart like the sound of a trumpet. 'Hear, O Viceroy, I spurn thy faith and I cleave to mine own. It is the way of our line to forfeit our life rather than our creed. . . . The torments inflicted by the Turks on our grandfather (Teg Bahadur) shall be the fire to consume them and our deaths shall be the wind to fan the flames. Thus shall we cleave to our faith and the Turks perish.'

The viceroy lost all self-control at this reply. He bade his servants take the boys away and kill them. They refused; but at last a Ghilzai Afghan offered himself as executioner. He took the poor little boys, one aged nine and the other seven and, like the cruel wretch that he was, slashed off their heads with a sword. Gujari died of grief and her body and those of her two grandsons were buried at the spot, where now rises the noble fane of Fatehgarh. I am glad to say that the treacherous Brahman did not profit by his villainy. The viceroy's police seized him and tortured him to find out where he had hidden Gujari's money. Someone had already stolen it from its hiding place and the Brahman could not say where it was. The sepoys did not believe him and tortured him until 'his soul took flight to the infernal regions.'

The cruel murder of the Guru's sons did the imperial cause no good. Aurangzib was far away in the Deccan, fighting a losing battle against the Maratha captains. In March 1707 he died, leaving a disputed inheritance. Bahadur Shah, the eldest son was at the time in Afghanistan. He hastened southwards; but before leaving the Punjab, he sought out Guru Gobind Singh and obtained his blessing and a promise of help. Bahadur Shah then marched against his two brothers and having defeated and killed them both, became emperor. The first request that Gobind Singh made of the emperor, whose communications he had kept open, was the surrender of Wazir Khan the viceroy of Sarhind. He frankly admitted that he intended to do unto the viceroy what the viceroy had done to the Guru's own children. The emperor dared neither to consent nor to refuse. He put off his decision and took the Guru with him on a march through the empire. The emperor hoped vainly that the Guru would forget the murder of his children. When the imperial army reached Nander the Guru went to the hut of one Madho Das, a Bairagi or hermit. In Madho Das' absence the Guru shot one of his goats and ate it. The hermit returned in a high rage; but Gobind Singh so convinced him of the truth of the Sikh tenets, that the hermit offered all his goats to the Guru and called himself Banda or the slave of the Guru. In Banda the Guru found a fitting weapon for the punishment of Wazir Khan and Sachanand. With a large body of Sikhs Banda went north, defeated Wazir Khan and killed him in single combat. In Sarhind Banda found the wicked Sachanand. The Sikhs fixed an iron ring in his nose and putting a rope through it, they led him through the streets. Every passer by struck the wretch with a shoe or a stick until he died.

The Guru did not live to hear of his enemies' downfall. One day the Guru was preaching at Nander, when an Afghan, Gul Khan by name, who had often listened to him, suddenly took offence at some words he had used. He drew his dagger and stabbed the Guru three times. The latter did not recover although the emperor sent his own surgeons to attend him. As Gobind Singh lay dying, the leading Sikhs asked him to name a successor. He refused saying :

> 'Henceforth the Guru shall be the Khalsa and the Khalsa shall be the Guru. I have infused the spirit both of my mind and body into the Granth Sahib and the Khalsa.'

Gobind Singh died in 1708 a year after Aurangzib, having reigned gloriously for thirty-three years. Shortly after his death he appeared to one of his disciples, who was a hermit. The disciple went to the mourning Sikhs and said, 'You think that the Guru is dead. I saw him this very morning on a bay horse. When I bowed to him, he said, "Come, O Hermit, let me behold thee. Happy am I that I have met thee at the last moment." I asked the Guru where he was going. He smiled and said that he was going to hunt in the forest. He carried a bow and his arrows were fastened round his waist.'

TWO MODERN TEACHERS OF INDIA

20. Keshab Chandra Sen

The founder of the Brahmo Samaj, a sect that has produced more able and learned men than any other in India, was the famous Ram Mohun Roy (Ramamohuna Rai). He was a Kulin Brahman of Bengal. At the age of twelve he went to study at Patna, where Sufi influences were active. At fifteen he had a difference with his father and began to wander about after the manner of Hindu ascetics. In A.D. 1828 he founded a group of learned men, calling it first the Brahmo Sabha and afterwards the Brahmo Samaj. In 1830 he went to England where he was received with great honour and respect, but he never returned to India to give her the fruits of his new experience. He died in Bristol in 1833.

Ram Mohun Roy had long ceased to be an orthodox Hindu. He did not believe in the Hindu pantheon or the transmigration of souls. His work was carried on by Dwarkanath Tagore and his son Debendranath Tagore. The man, however, who was to give a real force to the Brahmo Samaj was Keshab Chandra Sen (Kesava Chandra Sen). The ancestral home of this remarkable man was Garifa. It was then a country village on the banks of the Hugli : it is now a manufacturing town and bears the name of Goripore. But although Keshab Chandra Sen's family estate was at Garifa, he himself was born and passed the first eight years of his

KESHAB CHANDRA SEN

life at Calcutta. The family claimed descent from the ancient Sen Rajas, semi-mythical monarchs, who ruled at the time of Alexander the Great; in any case they were an ancient aristocratic house, who in the eighteenth century had fallen on evil days. Keshab's great grandfather was a poet called Gokul Chandra Sen, whose second son Ram Kamal, starting from a salary of eight rupees a month, rose by sheer ability to the Diwanship of the Bank of Bengal and a salary of two thousand rupees a month. He was a Vaishnava; and although he knew Ram Mohun Roy, he had little sympathy with him. Ram Kamal's second son Peary Mohun Sen was the father of Keshab. Peary died at the early age of thirty-four when Keshab was only ten. Keshab's mother Saroda Sundari was a remarkable woman, who long survived her son. It was from her that, by general belief, he inherited his talents. In 1838 Keshab was born. He spent the first eight years of his life, as I have said, in Calcutta. His collegiate career was not the success that his friends had anticipated. However, he finished his college course and returning home lived an ascetic life. He was greatly attracted by Christian teaching and took a strange interest in John the Baptist. In 1857 he came under the influence of Debendranath Tagore and of his son Satyendranath Tagore.[1] The same year he became a memebr of the Brahmo Samaj. Not long afterwards he had his first difference with his family. He refused the Vaishnava intiation that his family

[1] When the writer was a very junior civilian, he had the honour of serving under Satyendranath Tagore, then District Judge of Satara in the Bombay Presidency. The writer has the kindest recollections of that great gentleman.

customs demanded. He threw himself into the widow remarriage movement, earning his livelihood at the same time as a clerk in the Bank of Bengal.

In 1860 he published his first tracts and the same year he had a public controversy with a Christian missionary Mr. Dyson. They parted friends. Keshab began now to attract attention even in England, where he entered into correspondence with two well-known theists, Mr. Newman and Miss Frances Cobbe. In 1861 he founded the second English newspaper edited by an Indian, the *Indian Mirror*. In 1862 he was elected a minister of the Brahmo Samaj. His second quarrel with his family occurred about this time. They tried to prevent his taking his wife with him to stay with Debendranath Tagore; but efforts were in vain. Keshab left the family house and was excommunicated. He received, however, as his share of the family property a cheque for twenty thousand rupees.

The ministry of Keshab Chandra Sen had a great effect on the future of Bengal. Previously, educated Bengalis were becoming Christians in large numbers; but the eloquence of the new teacher diverted a large proportion of likely converts to Christianity into the Brahmo fold. A few Hindu ideas still lingered there, and in any case the Brahmo faith presented none of the difficulties of Trinitarian Protestantism. Unfortunately the fiery zeal of Keshab could not live in harmony with the aristocratic repose of Debendranath Tagore. In 1865 their differences became irreconcilable. A cyclone destroyed the Brahmo Samaj meeting house at Jorasanko. Keshab left Debendranath's Samaj and founded a new branch. The parent organization became known as the Adi Brahmo Samaj. Its offshoot called itself the Brahmo Samaj. The new foundation was very poor, but it had the faith that moveth mountains. In March 1866 Keshab Chandra Sen created a great sensation by a lecture on 'Jesus Christ, Europe and Asia.' The Christian missionaries who attended, began to have hopes of his speedy conversion ; but although Keshab often went near the brink, I doubt if he ever seriously thought of becoming a Christian. Christ attracted him as a teacher ; but Christianity repelled him as a foreign and exotic creed. Later in 1866 Keshab made a most successful tour through Eastern Bengal. He adopted the life of a religious mendicant and lived where and how he could. He suffered great hardships but he also achieved great successes. It was at this time that he adapted from his family faith Vaishnavism, its *Sanhitans* or hymns. He also borrowed from the wandering mendicants of Bengal their rude instruments, the *khole,* the *karatal* and the *ektara.* He thought, no doubt, that living like a mendicant, such instruments were his fitting companions. To his aid came in 1867 Trylokya Nath Sanyal, a famous singer. The latter composed new and beautiful hymns, while Keshab wrote a new liturgy for the rising sect. The funds collected on his tour enabled Keshab to build in 1868 the Brahmo Mandir, the new head quarters of his ministry. When the building was finished, the hymns were sung in it and the liturgy read. The same evening the Viceroy Lord Lawrence and most of the high officials of Calcutta attended the inauguration lecture. Yet another innovation followed and that was the *Nagar Sankirtan.* A great procession of Brahmos walked barefoot through the Calcutta streets, singing Keshab 's songs and led by Keshab in person. The town procession was a loan from Vaishnavism, but Keshab's processions were better organized. They created great enthusiasm among the youth of Calcutta.

In 1870 Keshab Chandra Sen resolved to go, as Ram Mohun Roy had done, to England. His followers did not approve; nevertheless he went. His tour in England was a triumph. Lord Lawrence was by that time in retirement in England and helped Keshab as well as he could. The great Brahmo preached first before Dr. Martineau and the Unitarians in Little Portland Street, then at an enormous gathering of all creeds in the Hanover Square Rooms. Mill, Gladstone, Lord Shaftesbury and Mr. Spurgeon all met him. The climax was reached when he was presented to Queen Victoria by the Duke of Argyll. He returned to India in October 1870 at the very height of his fame. This fame endured unassailed for seven years. Then the most unfortunate incident in his life occurred, namely the betrothal and marriage of Keshab's daughter to the young Maharaja of Kuch Behar.

Looking back on this event, it is hard for us to understand why it should have caused such an intense excitement. But the great success of Keshab had filled many of his followers with malice and envy. They seized at the chance afforded them by the marriage. The Maharaja of Kuch Behar was the head of a princely house in Bengal and, educated by an English teacher, had reached an age when he had to be given a bride. The English officials thought of Keshab's daughter. She was only fourteen and Keshab had advocated adult marriages. Nevertheless Keshab thought that the adherence of so great a family to the Brahmo Samaj might be worth some sacrifices. He consented to the marriage, provided that the bridegroom, who was a Hindu, became a Brahmo and that the marriage was celebrated according to Brahmo rites. Unfortunately at the ceremony, through the influence of the elder ladies of the Maharaja's household, some Hindu observances were introduced. Keshab protested, but he was powerless. As a matter of fact no harm had been done. The husband became and remained a Brahmo and the children were brought up as Brahmos. Nevertheless the marriage was the signal of a tremendous outburst.

Deeply grieved at the differences and at the same time deeply hurt with his following, Keshab led a new succession, which he styled the Nava Vidhana or the New Dispensation. The headquarters of this organization he erected close to his own home, Lily Cottage. He called it Nava Devalaya. This was in 1883. Unhappily Keshab Chandra Sen had contracted diabetes, caused no doubt by the cares and anxieties through which he had passed. His energy remained seemingly unaffected, but his health rapidly deteriorated. After a very painful illness he passed away on the morning of January 8, 1884. On his death all the quarrels that had embittered and shortened his life were hushed in admiration for the great preacher, whose eloquence was for ever stilled in death. English, Hindus, Brahmos and Musulmans alike gathered to do honour to the dead leader, as the funeral procession passed Beadon Park. The cremation of the body took five hours and its ashes were collected in an urn and brought back to Lily Cottage. Fifteen days later the ashes were deposited in front of the Nava Devalaya. A white marble obelisk marks the spot where lie the mortal remains of the man whose dynamic force made the Brahmo Samaj what it is to-day. On the obelisk are written the words 'Truth, Love, Holiness.' Underneath is a happy quotation from the great orator's own writings:

'Long since has the little bird "I" soared away from this sanctuary, I know not where, never to return again.'

TWO MODERN TEACHERS OF INDIA

21. Dayanand Saraswati

The last sketch in this book is that of the founder of the Arya Samaj. In the town of Tankara in the native state of Morvi in Kathiawar, lived a wealthy Audich Brahman banker known as Ambashankar. He was *jamadar* of the town and a money-lender. In 1824 a son named Mulshankar was born to him. The father saw that his boy was well educated according to the learning of the time and when Mulshankar was fourteen, he knew a great part of the Vedas and had a working acquaintance with Sanskrit. Mulshankar's life was that of an ordinary Brahman boy until one Mahashivratra day. It was an important festival of the god Shiva and his father who was a rigid Shaivite required his son to spend the night fasting and sleepless in Shiva's temple. Ambashankar who went with his son, fell asleep; but to the watching boy came doubts as to the truth of Hinduism. He saw a mouse creep out of its hole and run over and eat the offerings made by the faithful to the divinity. He felt that the Lord of Kailas must be something different from the Shiva, who according to the Brahmans ate food, yet could not guard it, who carried a trident and rode a stone bull.

Mulshankar awoke his father and told him his doubts. Ambashankar explained that the stone *Shivlinga* was not the god himself, but only his symbol. It had been consecrated by pious Brahmans and its use was to draw men's minds to the greatness and glory of the deity. The boy was not satisfied and this night is still spoken of by the boy's followers as 'Dayanand Bodha Utsava' or the spiritual awakening of Dayanand, the name by which, as will be seen, Mulshankar came to be known.

The doubts of which the seed had been sown, grew. They were strengthened, when Mulshankar was sixteen years old, by the deaths from cholera, of his younger sister and of his uncle, to both of whom he was devotedly attached. Ambashankar thought that it was high time that his son Mulshankar should marry and have done with religious speculation. Mulshankar begged for a respite and asked to be sent to Benares to study Astronomy and Physics. This prayer Ambashankar refused, but he sent Mulshankar to study under a local Pandit, who lived six miles from Morvi. The Pandit, however, found that his pupil's mind ran on metaphysics rather on science and he advised the celebration of his marriage as soon as possible. Mulshankar, unwilling to assume the responsibilities of married life, ran from his father's home. On the way he was robbed of his money by wandering mendicants, who, mocking him, they told him that this was a good preparation for abandonment of the world. Nothing daunted, the boy walked on until at last he met a *sanyasi* Lala Bhagat Ram by name, who initiated him into the order of the Naishti Brahmacharis and gave him the name of Shudha Chaitanya. A Brahmachari, however, is only a learner and Mulshankar wished for full initiation. Going towards Sidhapur in search of a teacher, he was recognized by a friend of the family. The friend sent word to Ambashankar that he had seen his fugitive son. The father started with some armed servants for Sidhapur and finding Mulshankar, seized him and would have dragged him home. The same night while his guards slept, the boy escaped and hid in a *pipul* tree. All next day his father with his armed servants searched for Mulshankar, but in vain. At last they gave up the search and left Sidhapur. Then only did the youth leave his tree.

From Sidhapur Mulshankar wandered about in search of an instructor in *Sanyas,* but in vain. The ascetics whom he met told him that he was too young for initiation. At last after waiting for a whole year on the banks of the Narbada River, he met a *Swami* from Maharashtra called Purnanand. Him Mulshankar asked for initiation ; but Purnanand hesitated because his *ashrama* or hermitage was in Maharashtra, whereas the youth was from Guzarat. At last Purnanand consented and gave him the staff of his order. He named him afresh Swami Dayanand Saraswati, by which title he was known thereafter. Dayanand was now twenty-four and for the next twelve years he wandered about India without finding any satisfactory solution of his religious difficulties. At last he reached Mathura and there met one of the most remarkable men who have ever lived. This was Swami Virajanand. A Saraswata Brahman of Gangapur, Virajanand was, as a child, called Sriman Narayan Dutt. Losing his eyesight through small-pox in his sixth year, he yet became the greatest Sanskrit scholar of his age. Left an orphan at eleven, he ran away into the forest and blind although he was, lived there for several years. Later he became a religious ascetic and received the name of Virajanand Swami. Employed as a tutor by the Maharaja of Ulwar, he resigned his post in a rage, because his pupil one day missed a lesson. He then made his way to Mathura. There he decided that religion was only to be found in the Vedas and in such Sanskrit books as were written before the Mahabharata. On meeting Virajanand, Dayanand asked that he might become his disciple. Virajanand consented and for two and a half years he taught Dayanand from the vast stores of his own Vedic learning. But the post of pupil to the hot tempered anchorite was no sinecure and many were the stripes that the unhappy Dayanand had to suffer before he finished his apprenticeship. When at last Virajanand dismissed his pupil, he gave him this parting message, 'Teach the people to study the true books, to believe in one God and in the religion taught by the Vedas.'

It was on these theistic lines that Dayanand conceived his mission. He first went to Agra, where he preached a number of sermons denouncing idolatry. He spoke in Sanskrit of which he was now a master; but that language was understood by so few, that he made little or no impression. From Agra he went to Gwalior and to Ajmir. In A.D. 1866 he went to Haridwar, where the Ganges issues from the Himalayas. It was the time of the Kumbhamela fair, held every twelve years, and in the presence of the assembled learning and nobility of India, he denounced the practices of orthodox Hinduism. The attack was a failure. Still speaking in Sanskrit, his words fell upon ears that had no understanding. He was not discouraged and in Cawnpore in July 1869 he challenged the orthodox Pandits to prove that the Vedas sanctioned idol worship. The Pandits took up the challenge and strangely enough the disputants chose as their umpire a young Englishman Mr. W. Thaire, then Joint Magistrate of Cawnpore. He had a great reputation as a Sanskrit scholar. After listening to the many and lengthy speeches, Mr. Thaire held that Dayanand had won the controversy and that it was not the Vedas, but the Puranas that approved of idol worship.

It was not, however, until A.D. 1872 when Dayanand met Keshab Chandra Sen in Calcutta that he achieved widespread success. At the Brahmo leader's advice, he began to preach in Hindi and not in Sanskrit. He also followed Keshab Chandra Sen's example by founding a society of his own to which he gave the name, now famous all over India, of the Arya Samaj. As the head of the Arya Samaj, Dayanand went to Poona; but the Deccan then, at any rate, would have none of him. The Punjab on the other hand welcomed the new teacher with open arms. From this time on, Dayanand's progress was from triumph to triumph. He enjoyed his victories for about ten years, but in A.D. 1883 death surprised him in Ajmir.

Whether he was right or wrong in his creed, it would be impertinent for a foreigner to say; but there is no doubt but that he was a man of the highest gifts. He had handsome features, a fine presence, a splendid voice and a stupendous memory. He condemned early marriages and advocated foreign travel. Indeed he maintained that

America was no other than the mysterious Patala of the Epics visited by several of the Aryan heroes. Dayanand was a vegetarian like most Hindus; but he had strange views about marriage. He held that neither man nor woman whose marriage had been consummated should marry again. If they could not remain chaste, they should beget children by Niyoga marriages, that is to say by temporary unions. Even some of his followers have styled this 'an anomalous practice.' The greatest tribute to his gifts is the vigour and strength of the movement that he created. The Arya Samaj is to be found everywhere in northern India and it has powerful branches in all other parts of India. It has grown apace and has deserved to do so. It has interested itself greatly in female education; and one of its leaders Lala Lajpat Rai has recently founded in Lahore a Vedic Salvation Army in the hope of helping outcastes after the manner of General Booth's organization. Whether the Arya Samaj will always be able to keep separate from orthodox Hinduism remains to be seen. Sooner or later Hinduism tends to gather to its bosom all Indian sects, just as the Ganges gathers to her bosom all the rivers of Hindustan.